THE ART OF THE FOLD

THE ART OF THE FOLD

How to Make Innovative Books and Paper Structures

Hedi Kyle and Ulla Warchol

LAURENCE KING PUBLISHING

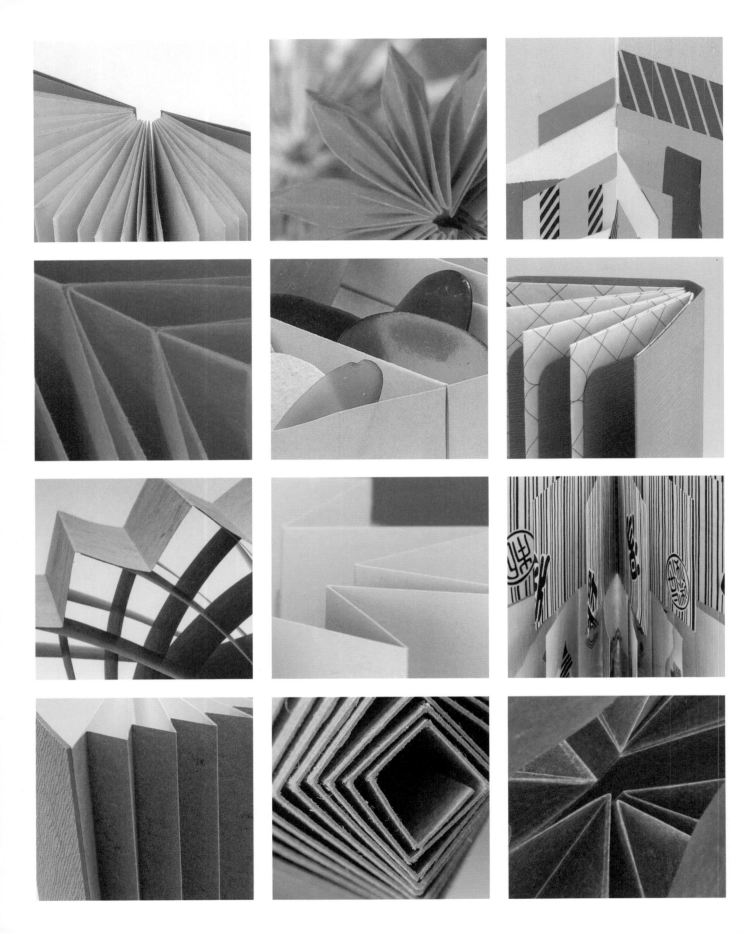

Preface

I can still remember the thrill I experienced when my first folded book structure emerged from my fingers – how eager I was to explore its possibilities and to share it with whoever was interested. The Flag Book, as I now call it, is a simple accordion and has interlocking pages oriented in opposite directions. Little did I know that this simple structure would have legs and be the catalyst for the next forty-plus years of thinking about and making books.

The common perception of the book today is fairly straightforward: a series of pages organized around a spine and protected on either side by two covers. This format allows for easy access, storage and retrieval of information. Yet what happens when the book is stripped away of centuries of preconceptions and is allowed to reveal something else: playfulness, utility, invention? Expanding the notion of the book is what the structures in the following chapters attempt to do. Exploring its tactile, sculptural form, primarily through folding methods, the book as a structural object is celebrated while content is considered in a new and unconventional way.

My range in this medium has always been broad. In part this is due to my introduction to the world of bookbinding and some chance encounters. In the 1970s in New York City, the art and craft of hand bookbinding and papermaking were experiencing an unprecedented revival. I was fortunate to arrive in the city at just this moment. With an art-school background and an impulse to make things, I was naturally drawn to pursue this new opportunity. The Center for Book Arts, the famous forerunner of so many centers yet to come, was located in a small storefront just down the street from where I lived on the Lower East Side of Manhattan. Under the direction of founder Richard Minsky, it had a radical mission: to push concept, materials, printing and making of artist books in a new direction. When Richard dared me to teach at the Center one evening a week, I was hooked.

An opportunity to study traditional binding and conservation in the studio of Laura S. Young, one of the preeminent teachers of bookbinding and conservation, exposed me to the fundamentals of bookbinding: sewing, backing, gilding, stamping, tooling and leather work. The Guild of Book Workers, located uptown – and philosophically much further away – offered a vast source of knowledge of craftsmanship, tools and techniques. Traveling between these two worlds, I became immersed in both, practicing tradition and following innovation. At night I would experiment in my studio with ideas and methods I was being exposed to. It was a time of reinvention – and paper, rather than leather, became my passion. It is the shaping, forming, folding and manipulation of paper that, to this day, keeps me so engaged.

My career as a book conservator and a book artist has now spanned over 45 years. As head conservator at the American Philosophical Society in Philadelphia, I've had the opportunity to handle some of the rarest volumes and manuscripts in the world. I have also dealt with decrepit books, torn maps and countless curiosities discovered in stacks and archives. All were endless sources for ideas and provided a springboard for a departure from tradition. Leading book-arts workshops around the world and a 25 year tenure teaching in the graduate program for Book Arts and Printmaking at the University of the Arts in Philadelphia have shown me, in retrospect, that the more I taught, the more it propelled me to experiment and develop my ideas. The many students I have had over the years were always my biggest inspiration, and they continue to be so.

"Are you writing a book?" This is a question I've heard many times and the idea had been percolating for some time. Devoting the time and focus necessary proved to be the biggest challenge. An email from Paul Jackson in the summer of 2016 started an encouraging correspondence and thanks to his gentle prompting and introducing me to his publishers at Laurence King Publishing, the writing of this book became a reality.

My daughter, Ulla, often with me in my studio while growing up, was always eager to create her own versions of what she saw me making. Over the years we have collaborated many times, teaching workshops, designing papers and making books. As the co-author of this book, she has been indispensable. We spent many a day talking in folds, often beginning by going over written instructions and drawings. Soon thereafter, paper would appear and folding would ensue, and by sundown the table would be covered with alternate versions at every scale. Several of the structures even earned the title "little devils," as they repeatedly eluded being boxed in and defined. With her architectural background and eye for detail, Ulla was able to distill inherent qualities in structures that previously had not been obvious to me. She transformed my hand drawings into images I could only hope for, improving on their clarity while retaining the gestural style I have developed over the years.

Finally, we collaborated with Ulla's husband, Paul Warchol, an architectural photographer who has been photographing my structures for years. His keen eye and critical lens, focused on our miniature assemblage of blizzards, fish bones and flags, has produced beautiful photographs to accompany each of the projects in this book.

Everything we show in this book has an inherent capacity for development in new directions. Unburdened by tradition, the projects in this book have no limits as to where, why and how they will be made or used. We can only hope that our collection of books and objects folded from paper will inspire you to jump in at any point and start folding!

Hedi Kyle, Pine Hill, NY
Sept 2017

Tools

A tool kit is gathered over time and is, as anyone who makes things on a regular basis can attest to, a highly personal curated collection. The tools used to accomplish the projects in this book are readily available, can be improvised in some cases and are all hand tools. Finding older, gently used versions that come with their own history at a flea market is a particularly serendipitous discovery. The internet offers an overwhelming assortment of options as well.

While it is ideal to have a board shear (paper cutter), a corner rounder or exquisitely hand-carved bone folders, cost, space and availability are important considerations. Thus we divide the list into two categories: essential and optional. We trust that you will have as much fun assembling these tools as you will have in using them. We begin with the most important...

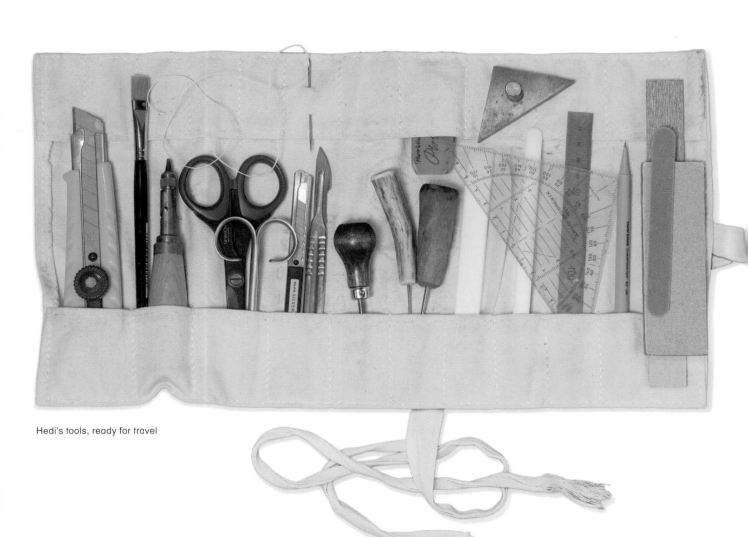

Hedi's tools, ready for travel

Essential tools

These are the tools we use every day. Most of the tools described can be found in art supply stores and are not specific to bookbinding. The good news is that most art supply stores increasingly also stock basic bookbinding tools. There are, as well, specialty purveyors that offer a broad array of hand bookbinding and conservation tools and equipment, and are often a good source for paper too. Hardware stores and sewing supply stores are other places to look for several of the tools listed below.

RULER/STRAIGHT EDGE
A good metal straight edge is ideal for cutting against. Cork-backed and heavy metal rulers are safest, as they tend not to slip or deflect the knife. For the projects in this book, an 18-in. (50-cm) and a 36-in. (1-m) ruler are recommended.

UTILITY KNIFE
A utility knife is a personal choice, but because most of the cuts involved in these projects are straight cuts, we recommend a knife with breakaway blades. Two sizes are ideal: a lightweight one for cutting paper and a heavy-duty one for cutting board. The constant supply of sharp blades allows one to follow the advice that a sharp blade is much safer than a dull one.

KITCHEN KNIFE
A kitchen paring knife is useful for cutting down large sheets of paper, especially when a paper cutter is not available.

SELF-HEALING CUTTING MAT
Choose one that is imprinted with a grid and of a size convenient for you. The ideal situation is to set up a fairly large mat on which to cut, score, crease and fold.

TRIANGLE
Collect a variety of sizes. A large, see-through, right-angle triangle is useful for squaring paper. A metal triangle provides a cutting edge as well as a squaring edge. Small triangles are useful when squaring up small cuts.

CLEAR PLASTIC GRIDDED RULER
Marked in inches or centimeters, this assists in alignment and allows you to measure distances between parallel lines. Its transparency lets you see what is underneath.

BONE FOLDER OR TEFLON FOLDER
Used to score, flatten creases, burnish and smoothen surfaces. We recommend having both a thin, pointed one made from bone and a broad, rounded one made from Teflon. Bone folders are strong and exact; Teflon folders are less rigid and leave no markings on the work.

AWL
A sharp-pointed metal shaft set into a wooden handle is ideal for making marks and small holes. A needle stuck into a cork works in a pinch. However, consider collecting a number of awls ranging in size and sharpness of the point, as they can pierce different sizes of holes.

SCISSORS
Both large and small scissors are handy to have, but small ones are recommended for finer details and cutting off double-sided tape from the roll. Most of the cutting necessary in our instructions, however, is best achieved with a utility knife.

WEIGHTS/PRESSING BOARDS
Many things can be utilized as weights: wrapped bricks, antique non-electric irons, cans filled with coins, rocks, barbells and, last but not least, heavy books. Weights are used to hold things in place and to avoid shifting. In combination with pressing boards (made from plywood, hardwood or masonite), they keep the work flat while drying after parts have been pasted.

BRUSHES
A variety of brushes is useful: natural bristle for wheat paste, polyester bristle for PVA, and a small, flat detail brush for paint or for working in tight areas.

SANDING BLOCK/EMERY BOARD
A sanding block can be made by gluing a piece of sandpaper to a flat piece of wood or heavy, dense cardboard. A different grit (fine and rough) can go on each side. For small areas, emery boards, found in the nailcare section of a pharmacy, are also useful.

NEEDLES
Darning or tapestry needles are best, as their points are slightly dulled so they don't split the sewing thread while sewing.

PAPER CLIPS/BULLDOG CLIPS
These are handy to keep in any tool kit. There are many occasions where they truly make all the difference and hold things together.

PENCILS AND ERASERS
Pencils should be sharpened for accuracy but of soft, erasable lead weights (H and softer). Choose erasers that are kind to paper surfaces.

Optional tools

These tools are not essential to accomplish the projects contained in this book. They do, however, make the work easier and in some cases elevate the quality of the finished product. If you become inspired to do more projects with books and with paper in general, they may be worthwhile investments.

PAPER CUTTER

Many paper cutters and trimmers (also called board shears) exist in the market. The best ones have a clamp or pressure bar to hold a sheet of paper or board firmly in position while making a cut, ensuring a square result. These cutters are expensive and take up a substantial amount of room. They are a dream to use if available, but not necessary for the work described in this book.

KEY STOCK

These are thin flat strips of brass or aluminum that are approximately 12 to 20 in. (30 to 50 cm) in length. They come in widths that increase by regular increments and are available in both the metric and US customary systems. They substitute for a measurement normally made with a ruler. Not a traditional bookbinding tool, they are found in hobby shops and hardware stores, and now more increasingly in art supply stores. Collect an assortment of widths ranging from ¼ to 2 in. (0.5 to 5 cm). If key stock is not available, cut exact strips in the range of widths/units you are likely to use most from thin, rigid pressboard for scoring and measuring purposes.

HOLE PUNCHES

A Japanese push drill has a twist drill mechanism, allowing you to drill through paper easily and even through dense binder's board. A set includes a variety of interchangeable tips delivering a range of (circular) diameters from miniscule to ample. A less expensive option is a mini punch set with interchangeable tips that is used with a mallet rather than a hammer.

CORNER ROUNDER

Corner rounders are very simple manual punching machines that remove the sharp corners of pages, covers and cards. In the past they were used primarily in the book conservation and library fields to prevent "dog-earing". They were very expensive, especially if you wanted several diameter options for the corners. However, with the advent of scrapbooking, corner rounders are available at all price points and quality levels from major arts and crafts stores. Is quality a concern? You're punching the corner off a piece of paper – how difficult can that be? Go for it!

GOUGES

Traditionally used for carving by woodworkers, these are ideal for punching out thumb notches, shaping slits to secure pictures on an album page or preventing a slot from tearing. We've even used them to create pop-up shapes. Gouges can be found in fine hardware stores and catalogs. There are many varieties of U-curves and V-shapes available. Sharpness is the name of the game here.

EMBOSSING STYLUS

Often found in sets of three with dual-tips, the embossing stylus is a versatile tool that can be used for scoring.

BOX CORNER ASSEMBLY

One of the most helpful tools we've used is an assembly comprised of a wooden board and two aluminum L-squares attached to the edges of the board, creating a 90-degree corner. A cutting mat fits into this corner, making it perfect for measuring and cutting materials straight and square. Additionally, used in combination with key stock, the fixed angle provides a stable edge against which to make one or multiple score lines. As far as we know, these are not commercially available – we encountered it at Daniel Kelm's Wide Awake Garage in Northampton, Mass., many years ago and have since been making our own. If you are a book artist and work on many projects including small editions, you will find it extremely helpful. A perfectly adequate alternative to this is to clamp a metal angle to the edge of your worktable.

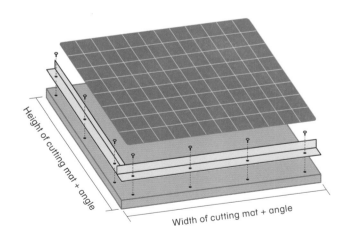

Height of cutting mat + angle

Width of cutting mat + angle

Ulla's tools, ready for studio work

Materials

In this section we discuss how to make appropriate paper selections, adhesives and a few other materials you will encounter in this book. We also provide a list of sources for the papers we used in creating the models, though we encourage you to experiment with what is readily available in your part of the world.

Papers

Nothing is more important than paper with regards to our folded structures. The papers we chose for our models have been tested in many workshops and have proven to be especially well suited for folding. You may have favorites among the huge selection offered, and a lot depends on availability and cost. As a general rule, we feel that the paper needs to be of high quality and, above all else, it has to fold well. When practicing you can get away with inferior paper — but on the other hand think about your skills, and the time you invest. Part of that experience is the tactile and cooperative interaction with the materials. Through folding you quickly develop a feel for paper and its inherent capacity to be transformed. The scale of our models is small; nevertheless, you will be surprised how often you start out with a good-sized piece of paper. Folding reduces dimensions quite quickly! One project calls for a 5-ft- (1.5-m-) long piece of paper and therefore our advice would be to look for paper on a roll wherever possible.

DETERMINING GRAIN DIRECTION

The grain direction in paper is the result of the fiber line-up when paper is manufactured. Parallel with the fibers, the paper will bend without resistance, curl when wet, fold nicely and tear evenly. In the direction against the grain or in the cross-grain direction, the paper's behavior is not so accommodating. In the worst scenario, it will crack when folded and barely bend. As a general rule, the paper grain should run in the direction parallel to the spine of books, folders, boxes and wrappers. We follow this rule and you will see the grain direction symbols throughout the book, especially at the start of a project when the components are introduced. We underline the dimension that should run parallel with the grain in the table provided for each project. Since many of our models are folded from one sheet of paper, folds are inevitably running in both directions, and folding against the grain is unavoidable. Therefore we chose papers that allow this kind of diversity and fold well in both directions.

PAPER WEIGHT

The many different ways the weight of paper is referred to in catalogs and on websites seems confusing and often inconsistent, and perhaps not worth describing here in detail. We are dealing with creative book objects with a capacity for development through trial and error. The weight of the paper used will indeed affect their movement and aesthetics, but we suggest that you get to know the weight of paper through touch and feel rather than through an abstract numbering system. In each project we provide an appropriate weight of paper to use, followed by what we actually used. We are confident that, with some experience, you will make great choices of your own.

PAPER EQUIVALENTS

These are our suggestions for paper weights matched with the papers we used, all of which are readily available.

LIGHTWEIGHT PAPER	Japanese papers: Obonai Feather, Tatami, Dai Chiri, Mulberry Handmade paper Tracing paper Found or recycled paper
TEXT-WEIGHT PAPER	French Speckletone 70T French Dur-O-Tone 70T French Parchtone 60T Fabriano CMF Ingres 90 gsm Elephant hide paper 110 gsm Borden & Riley #840 Kraft Paper Japanese Momi paper, 90G [i.e. 90 gsm] Topographic and navigational maps
COVER-WEIGHT PAPER	Elephant hide paper 190 gsm Vegetable parchment French Speckletone 80C French Dur-O-Tone 80C Handmade Zaansch bord
CARDSTOCK	Japanese linen cardstock, 244g [i.e. 244 gsm]
BOARD	Davey Red Label Binder's Board .060 Pressboard
PAPER ON A ROLL	Butcher paper Wrapping paper Glassine Tyvek Mylar Chart paper

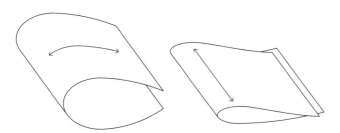

Paper sources

These are our sources – there are many others. Paper weight is listed in the same way it appears either in the catalog or on the website of the company from which it was sourced. Please note that we designed the patterned papers that appear in this book and had them custom printed on the French paper. These patterns are not available from the French Paper Co.

Elephant Hide, by Zanders, 27⅕ x 39⅛ in.,110 gsm, 190 gsm
Fabriano CMF Ingres, 39½ x 27½ in. , 90 gsm
DuPont Tyvek
Davey Binder's Board
Mylar
Glassine
3M #415 double-sided tape
Available from Talas
www.talasonline.com

FRENCH PAPER
Construction, 12½ x 19 in., 80 cover, 70 text
Dur-O-tone, 12½ x 19 in., 80 cover, 70 text
Speckletone, 12½ x 19 in., 80 cover, 70 text
Parchtone, 12½ x 19 in., 65 cover, 60 text

Available from the French Paper Company
www.frenchpaper.com

JAPANESE PAPER
Japanese linen cardstock, 43 x 31 in. Grain (43") 244g
Tatami Orange, #253 50 gsm, 25 x 37 in.
Momi 90G

Available at fine paper stores or from
The Japanese Paper Place
www.japanesepaperplace.com

HANDMADE PAPER
Zaansch bord from the Netherlands made from rags by wind papermill De Schoolmeester in Westzaan
deschoolmeester@hetnet.nl

KRAFT PAPER, PAPER ON A ROLL, PATTERNED PAPERS
Available at fine paper and art supply stores.

Other useful materials

WASTE PAPER
Keep newsprint and waxed paper near your working area to protect your work in general and particularly when using adhesive. Newsprint is also handy to practice folding or to make a quick model to study a technique (see Gluing and Pressing, page 25).

THREAD
We sewed the Tree Fold (pages 112–15) into the Diagonal Pocket fold with Barbour linen No. 35/3 and the Spider Book (pages 136–40) with No. 18/3. Barbour linen may be replaced with thread you have; just make sure it is strong and won't break when pulled taut.

Adhesives

In the projects presented here, we seldom use adhesives. When we do, we are confident in the archival nature and bonding ability of the following:

PASTE
Paste is ideal for adhering large areas of paper to board. It can easily be prepared at home using rice starch, wheat starch or even flour.

Recipe: In a small saucepan add ¼ cup of cold water to 4 tablespoons of rice starch and whisk until the starch is completely dissolved. Keep whisking while adding ½ cup of boiling water. Place the saucepan over a low heat, stirring the paste until it thickens and turns translucent. Let it boil for one minute, remove from the heat and pour the paste into a bowl to cool. Stir occasionally to prevent a skin from forming. Paste can be thinned with cold water. It does not have a long shelf life and prolonged refrigeration will make it watery and less effective. It is best to make paste in small batches as you need it.

PVA ADHESIVE/JADE GLUE
Straight PVA is a strong adhesive, but dries very fast and is difficult to handle when gluing large areas. We recommend its use for small areas that need to bond immediately.

MIXTURE
Mix methyl cellulose following the directions on the package. By itself it does not have much adhering strength and is best mixed with PVA, in a 60:40 ratio (methyl cellulose:PVA) to the consistency of heavy cream.

DOUBLE-SIDED TAPE
We refer to the archival 3M #415 double-sided tape backed with a strip of release paper. Once you put the tape down on one side, you can take your time positioning the part to be adhered before peeling off the release paper strip. There are other double-sided tapes on the market, some without the protective strip. These are less expensive and will work, though they give you less room for error. We highly recommend using an archival tape and one with a paper backing. Be sure to store double-sided tape in a plastic zip-lock bag, as it can attract unwanted particles of dust and lint.

Terminology

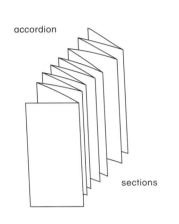

accordion

sections

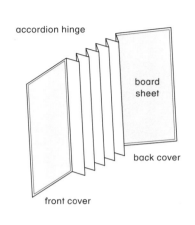

accordion hinge

board sheet

back cover

front cover

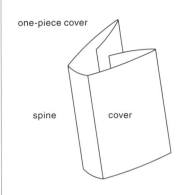

one-piece cover

spine

cover

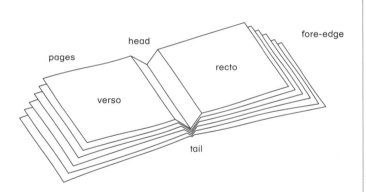

head

pages

fore-edge

recto

verso

tail

inside reverse folding

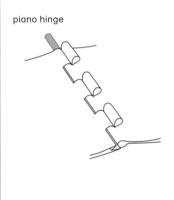

piano hinge

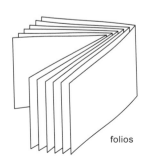

folios

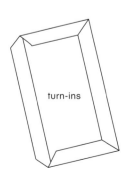

turn-ins

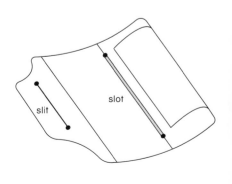

slit

slot

Symbols

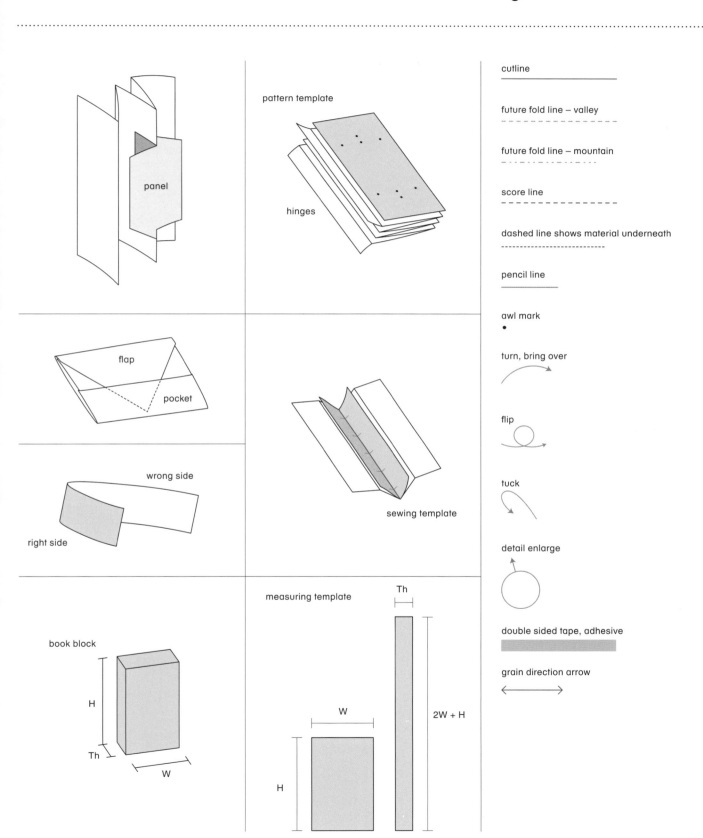

panel

pattern template

hinges

flap

pocket

wrong side

right side

sewing template

book block

H

Th

W

measuring template

Th

W

H

2W + H

cutline

future fold line – valley

future fold line – mountain

score line

dashed line shows material underneath

pencil line

awl mark

•

turn, bring over

flip

tuck

detail enlarge

double sided tape, adhesive

grain direction arrow

Techniques

The irony of this section on techniques appearing at the beginning of this book is that we wrote it last. We made, discussed, remade, drew, redrew and photographed all the models contained in this book before we arrived at the fundamental techniques included here. These techniques evolved through years of Hedi's studio practice, as well as teaching hands-on in college courses and workshops. Some of them have been eureka moments in the studio, others have come from encounters with people who do things a little differently and new tricks have been incorporated – we call those ones "the price of admission". We love to read similar sections in books on bookbinding and paper folding – also called "methods", "how to use this book", "helpful hints", etc. – as inevitably there are discoveries to be made.

The nature of Hedi's way of working is intuitive and, as you will discover, does not rely heavily on the use of rulers. That is not to say there isn't measuring or math involved! Some techniques appear often, some just once or twice. If they are tricky and need a little background, we include it here. We hope these techniques will be useful to you and can be applied to other projects you may encounter in paper folding and bookmaking.

Marking

Marks are guides to indicate where to draw a line, score, fold or cut. We use three kinds of marks. The most spontaneous one is just a pinch with your fingernail to mark the middle of a sheet of paper or to measure a dimension (on a scrap of paper) for transfer. A pencil is used when we need a longer mark to guide us. Use a sharp and easily erasable pencil. The disadvantage of pencil marks is that they are only visible on one side of the paper. For that reason, as well as for more accuracy, we use an awl. Awl marks are precise, and they appear both in front of and on the back of the material, which is very helpful. Awl marks can mark a location through several layers of paper, perfectly registered. If that is not the desired intention, insert a piece of cardboard to protect the lower layers. When no longer in use, awl marks can be flattened with a bone folder and, for the most part, disappear. Consider the size of the awl's point when making marks – small ones for a temporary mark, larger ones for permanence or for sewing.

Dimensions

Throughout this book, we give dimensions in inches and in centimeters (US customary units/metric system). The conversion between the two systems is not meant to be exact. We have tested the models using both systems and have arrived at round numbers that consequently produce models of slightly different dimensions. Choose the system you are most comfortable with and follow that system exclusively, as they are not necessarily interchangeable. For the purpose of giving clear instructions, we suggest initial dimensions for each project (in both systems) as a jumping-off point.

Scaling proportions up or down

Many of these structures can be freely enlarged or reduced in scale to become tall and skinny or small and chunky by changing the relationship of the height and width of the initial sheet of paper. Some structures are, however, locked into a system that only works if the proportion (ratio) of height to width is kept in the same relationship, regardless of the size of the initial sheet of paper. A further investigation into folding paper and its proportional breakdowns into subdivisions has surprising geometrical outcomes. We encourage you to experiment with the sizes given before scaling the size of a structure up or down. In each of the chapters, advice is offered regarding the proportions of individual structures when necessary.

Measuring devices

Enclosures and wrappers that are designed to fit around a book or object need initial dimensions taken from the item itself. We prefer to use templates or paper strips instead of rulers to represent height, width and thickness. For this purpose, keep scraps of paper and cardstock handy.

PAPER STRIPS

Using a strip of paper, start by making a perpendicular fold near the end and stand it up. This right-angle corner will keep your book or object stationary while you measure the height, thickness or width. Mark the strip with a pinch mark, pencil mark or awl mark. Then place the strip on your sheet and transfer these measurements.

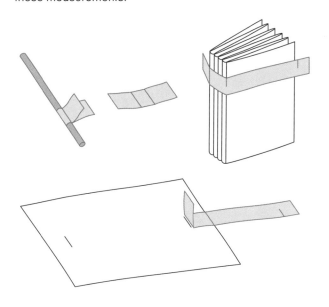

TEMPLATES

We employ two types of templates: those used for measuring and those used to transfer a pattern. To make a measuring template, place your item on a piece of cardstock. Mark the height and width. Be generous – add 1/16 in. (2 mm) when you're doing this. Cut the template out and repeat the process to make the spine template. Set your item aside and work only with the templates.

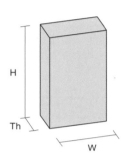 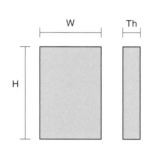

A pattern template can be used to layout and then transfer a pattern onto your work. Cut a piece of cardstock to the size of your work, do your layout on this card and transfer the resulting pattern by piercing holes through the template at strategic points onto a page, cover or sewing jig using an awl.

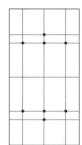 

SPACERS

A spacer is needed to size an enclosure accurately, accounting for the paper thicknesses of the enclosure itself. Glue together two or three pieces of the same material you are using for your project. These will become spacers. Use them when you make your measurements and need to add some extra card or paper thicknesses for ease and a better fit.

Centering a spine

Locating a spine dimension exactly in the center of a pre-cut cover sheet using a ruler can be challenging. This technique takes that anxiety away and is even slightly magical. It also makes it easier to fold a narrow spine. Transfer the spine thickness measurement to both edges of the cover piece. Bring the left side over to the right mark, press down and crease. Repeat by bringing the right side over to the left mark. The technique can be further employed to center a measurement of any size on the page. We use this technique quite often in this book and hope you will incorporate it into your own bag of tricks.

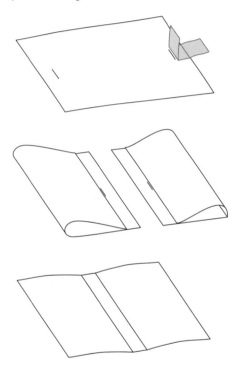

Cutting and trimming

A paper cutter or board shear is the ideal tool for cutting paper, but do not be discouraged if you need to use a knife and straight edge. Almost all of our projects are made from materials that are easy to cut. Using sharp blades is essential to obtaining straight cuts. If the material is thicker, it is better and safer to make a number of lighter cuts against a steel straight edge, taking care not to move it. Always cut on a self-healing mat or other protective surface. Scissors are useful for trimming small areas but less so for making long, straight cuts.

Using key stock, triangle and box corner assembly for measuring, scoring and squaring paper

The usefulness of this combination is one of the major factors liberating us from rulers. The upright angles of the box corner provide a stable wall against which to set a triangle, ensuring square cuts. Key stock makes marking a fold or a series of folds easy by using an assortment of widths. When set against the wall of the box corner, marking lines, score lines and cuts can all be achieved against the metal edge of the key stock. A very good alternative to the box corner is simply to clamp an angle to the edge of your table. (See further discussion of these in Tools, pages 8–11.)

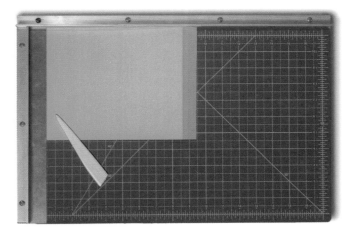

Dividing into an odd number of sections

It is fairly straightforward to divide a sheet of paper into an even number of sections – but what about an odd number? Successfully divide a piece of paper into three equal parts by making an S-curve and pinching the three topsides together after you have aligned them. Or, taking advantage of the printed grid on self-healing cutting mats, you can divide a piece of paper into three, five, seven or more uneven-number sections. On the gridded surface, count the same number of sections of the divisions you plan to make – we give an example for five sections below. Place the paper diagonally across the area between the first and last sections and make a mark at each intersection where the paper crosses the line. After dividing a sheet of paper into five equal parts, follow the diagram to make the folds.

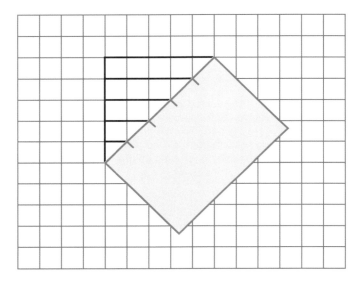

dividing into thirds

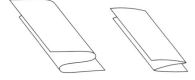

dividing into fifths

Squaring paper

Large sheets of paper or cardstock should be rough cut to approximate sizes so that you can handle them comfortably. Fold the desired amount over and make a sharp crease. Insert a kitchen knife into the fold and cut away from you with a sweeping motion. Next you will need to square cut the paper. By square cutting, we don't mean cutting it into a square – just that all the corners are at 90 degrees. In order to obtain a squared piece of paper, a large triangle is an essential tool.

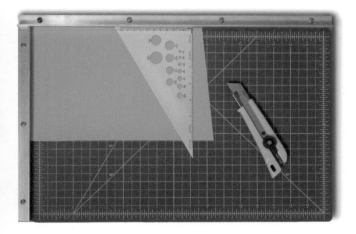

Cutting angles, darts and slivers

Angled cuts take care of any protruding material visible at corners and turn-ins. Darts are small wedge-shaped cuts that remove slivers of paper on either side of a fold to allow turn-ins to lie flat and not bunch up against the fold.

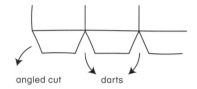

angled cut   darts

Accordion sections are joined together by attaching the last or first section of one accordion to the hinged section of the next. A narrow sliver is cut away from the section that attaches to the hinge to achieve a better fit and to avoid creep at the fore-edge.

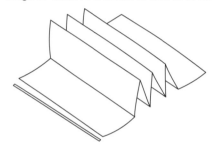

Making non-tear slits with anchor holes

A slit is just a single cut, whereas a slot uses two parallel cuts and the paper in between them is removed. Both slits and slots can be anchored in small holes for an enhanced appearance and to prevent tearing. The holes are made with a hole punch or an awl. We prefer the hole punch because it removes the small paper circle, whereas the awl hole needs to be flattened on the back. A small half-circle or U-gauge can also be used to inhibit tearing.

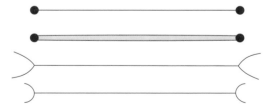

Rounding corners and thumb notches

The raw corners cut from cardstock are sharp and pointy and cause dog-ears – those bent, delaminated, used-to-be-crisp corners. Though we love books that are lovingly used, to prevent dog ears, soften the corner by trimming it into a rounded shape. This can be done using a corner rounder, or by hand after tracing them using a coin. Sometimes it is enough to just snip off the corner point and ease it with a piece of sandpaper. To cut a thumb notch, we recommend a U-shaped woodworking gouge and mallet, or tracing a coin and using a small scissor.

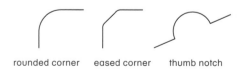

rounded corner   eased corner   thumb notch

Folding

As used in this book, the terms "scoring", "folding" and "creasing" describe the process of producing a fold that raises a flat surface to the third dimension and has the ability to expand and collapse. Scoring prepares the paper to be turned over or under; folding elevates the scored portions; and creasing sharpens the folds.

There is no way around it: precision is the key to successful folds! Embarking with squarely cut paper is the first step. Work with your paper in front of you and fold away from you against a dark background, so that you can see when the edges align. Slide your thumbs toward the middle of the intended fold and, pressing down, move your thumbs sideways in both directions. Use the bone folder to sharpen the fold. Once paper is folded, it is almost impossible to reverse it to its pristine stage. Think about an unintentional fold and the effort it takes to smoothen it out, let alone to make it disappear! Paper has memory, and the memory of the fold will always dictate the return to the paper's collapsed form.

SCORING WITH A BONE FOLDER

The bone folder is the bookmaker's most foundational tool, and is used to score paper and cardstock. Depending on what it is made of and whether its tip is pointed or rounded, firm or hard, a multitude of effects can be achieved with this amazing tool. Scores made with bone folders are sympathetic to the paper: they compress the fibers, but don't scratch or break the surface.

For very precise folds, use a bone folder with a pointed tip or a folder made out of metal. When using an actual bone folder, be aware that the bone can leave a shiny mark on the paper. To avoid this, use a protective scrap piece of paper between the bone folder and the work, or use a Teflon folder that does not leave marring marks.

When working with heavier paper or thin board, it is advisable to score along the desired fold line on top of the paper. Keeping the metal straight edge firmly in place, lift up the paper and run the bone folder underneath, pressing the paper against the straight edge. This effectively pre-creases the paper so that, when you finish off the fold, it is surprisingly cooperative.

MOUNTAIN AND VALLEY FOLDS

Origami has been, and continues to be, very influential in our work. Mountain and valley folds, the modus operandi for all things folded, play a big role. Understanding their relationship and how they operate will result in successful folding. Mountain and valley folds depend on the viewing angle. Turning the paper over reverses them – they become the other and behave differently. A series of folds moving in the wrong direction may present an obstacle, though keep in mind that folds can almost always be reversed without too much trouble. Rather than use abstract symbols, we have drawn our instructions with an indication of the direction of a fold, reflecting the flexible nature of paper.

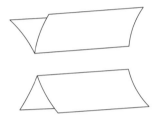

INSIDE REVERSE FOLD

The inside reverse fold is a combination of mountain and valley folds. It involves two layers of paper. The diagram below shows two variations. Both are inside reverse folds, sharing the same instructions. One begins at a corner of the paper folded to a point, while the other one uses a square corner. Crease the fold well and then lift. Separate the two layers of paper and spread them apart. Push the tip of the triangle, a mountain fold, into the gap created. Bring them together and crease to flatten the inside reversed triangle. This helpful fold is also used to make square ends smaller when they have to fit into pockets.

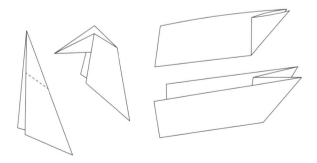

SQUASH FOLD

A squash fold begins with a triangle folded over and then unfolded. The two layers of paper are separated, spread to the sides and flattened. The angles to the right and left are equal and the crease in the middle, which was formerly the folded edge, now lines up nicely in its new central position. The squash fold is represented in the Diagonal Pocket fold (pages 116–19).

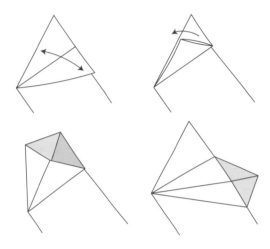

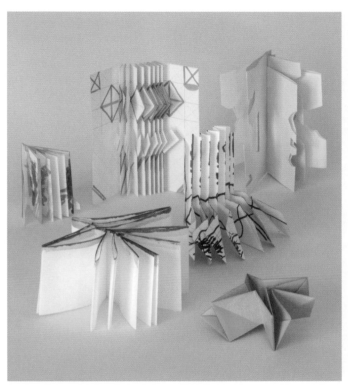

ROLLING FOLDS

Rolling sections over and over as you fold adds a little extra dimension to each consecutive section so that they lie flat and are not bunched up. Simply roll and gently press for slightly rounded folds or score and crease each time. This is a folding method that works best for covers, wrappers and envelopes. The rolling fold method, with its sequence of valley folds only, is best represented by our Telescoping Ziggurat (pages 162–65), but makes cameos in other places as well.

KNIFE PLEATS AND BOX PLEATS

The distances between mountain and valley folds are not regularly spaced in knife and box pleats. In this way they differ from the evenly spaced accordion fold and its ability to collapse into a compact pile. We use knife pleats to create pockets for our Diagonal Pocket fold (pages 116–19) and School-Book Wrapper with Pleat (pages 172–75). The box pleat can have a wonderful airiness to it and a variation is utilized in the pages of our Fishbone and Tree folds (pages 108–11 and 112–15).

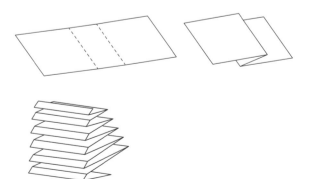

Sewing

There are only two projects in this book that employ sewing. That said, we believe it to be a necessary technique: one causing much anxiety yet quite simple to master. It is a technique that can be employed in a multitude of ways once experimenting with book structures is underway. Therefore, we provide some simple directions.

PREPARING A SEWING TEMPLATE

Making a sewing template (sometimes referred to as a jig) takes the guessing out of sewing. Rather than marking up your pages, make a template in advance before a single hole is made:

Cut a 3-in. (8-cm) strip of paper to the exact height of your book body, then fold it in half.

Fold the open-ended sides over by approximately 3/8 in. (1 cm).

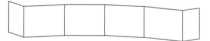

Fold the remaining section in half. Crease both folds well.

Unfold the strip.

Fold the strip in half lengthwise.

Mark the intersections of the folds with pencil lines.

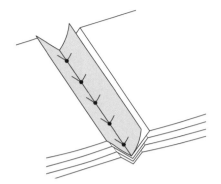

Nestle the strip into the spine fold of a page section (signature) and with an awl or sharp needle pierce holes through the pages at the marks.

SEWING FOLIOS

Thread a needle with thread about three times as long as the height of your book. Use a needle with a dull point, as you don't want to make new holes other than the ones pierced with your template. Start on the inside, entering through the middle hole. Leave a tail of about 3 in. (8 cm). Do not make a knot, rather hold on to the end or secure it with a piece of low-tack tape. Continue to sew, following the arrows of the diagram. Exit at the same hole where you started. Position the long middle stitch between the two ends. Pull gently at both ends of the thread to tighten the sewing and make a square knot.

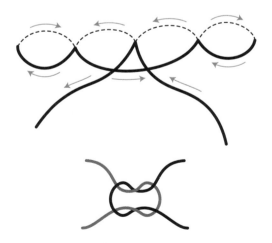

Covers

The models described in this book take a non-traditional, and even minimalist, approach when it comes to their covers. Issues to consider are both visual and technical: making structures lighter, able to stand and become instruments of display, pleasing to hold or to fit comfortably into one's pockets. Beauty is important: the choices made on the outside reflect what lies within, regardless of what the old adage says!

The accordion has always been at the very core of Hedi's work and, as such, folding long strips of paper inevitably led to inventing ways to make the covers a continuation of the folding process and not a separate component. Stiff covers are recommended for books that are going to be viewed standing up or for books that need covers to protect and add rigidity to very thin pages.

The flexible covers encountered in this book fall into two categories. The first are those made of one piece of cover paper, featuring spine folds to accommodate thickness and help to contain the contents within. The second are made from two separate sheets of cover paper, folded in half and attached to hinge extensions, operating independently and allowing the book to fully expand.

There are some projects in the following chapters that do not need or require covers. Made out of stiff paper, they function quite well on their own or are designed to be sculptural objects much more alive in their three-dimensional form than hidden away between covers. Wrappers, slipcases and envelopes are an ideal way to house these types of structures. They can live outside of them but nonetheless have a place for safekeeping.

We are confident that after making a variety of covers, you will begin to interchange and adapt them and even invent your own versions.

Use of adhesive when preparing stiff covers

Adhesive is used sparingly throughout this book, but it is essential in laminating paper to board. In the Flag Book (pages 54–58), we took a different approach to the traditional wrapped boards most commonly found in bookbinding. We sanded and painted the edges with a bright red, and then laminated the boards with a patterned paper. Consider collaging covers with bits of recycled, patterned or torn paper. The paper can extend beyond the edges of boards. After they have dried, sand away the excess. Wax or any other protective coating may then be applied.

Often when making stiff covers, we look for a material that already has a gorgeous texture or color of its own and doesn't require covering. The covers of the Two-Sided Flag Book (pages 59–61) are an example of this – recycled pressboard from an old notebook cover that is dense, strong but also thin, and a brilliant blue that defies obscuring with paper.

GLUING AND PRESSING

It is best to use paste when adhering paper to boards. Paste is easy to handle, it doesn't leave hard-to-remove spots and its slow drying time gives you time to turn in corners and sides. Mixture, made of PVA glue and methyl cellulose, is recommended if you are using a book cloth to cover boards (see Adhesives, page 13). Always apply paste or mixture to the paper rather than to the board. Protect your work surface when applying adhesives. Let the paper stretch and relax before centering the board on top of it.

Boards covered with paper only on one side will warp. To counteract warping, and after attaching the hinges of the spine to the boards, brush out a board sheet with paste. The board sheet is a sheet of paper, slightly smaller than the cover itself, adhered to the inside of the cover. It can be the same as the outer paper used or a different color of similar weight to add contrast. Place your covers between waxed paper, newsprint and pressing boards. Waxed paper does not stick and newsprint absorbs moisture and shortens the drying time. Weigh your boards down with a wrapped brick or a stack of books and let dry. The longer you leave it, the better – even overnight.

1
The Accordion

The Accordion

Just as the name implies, accordion folds are named after the musical instrument that effectively operates by contracting and expanding mountain and valley folds. As a book form, the accordion has achieved high status for centuries in countries like Japan, China and Korea. The subtle beauty and lightness of Asian papers contributes to its success. In the Western world the accordion book is encountered as a useful format with unequaled potential, as it is able to stand up on its own displaying a continuous array of pages or a fantastic panorama. It can be viewed in different ways – two pages at a time or in one long spread. This is of great advantage for display purposes where the accordion can also be viewed from the front and the back. It lies completely flat when opened – a characteristic not found in many books.

Throughout the chapters, we use the term "accordion" rather than switching back and forth among the other names you will most likely encounter: concertina, leporello, zigzag, fold book, fan book, folded binding, screen folds, Orihon and Sutra binding. While some of these terms indicate their origin and represent a specific style or purpose, many are being used interchangeably today. The accordion's physical presence is everywhere. We are increasingly fascinated by the playful mechanical function of the zigzag.

The accordion fold as an independent component is our focus point in this book. It is one of the most versatile ingredients in making books and its possibilities are endless. We have embraced the accordion fold for decades and discovered many varieties. In this book we are pleased to introduce to you a selection of our favorites. Let us start with a brief visual display of a variety of folding styles. Hopefully they will inspire you to grab some paper and start folding!

The accordion, in its most fundamental form, is created by folding a sheet of paper into uniform-sized sections. This diagram includes some terminology that we will use in the following chapters.

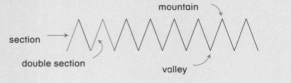

By folding a pattern of one small and one large section, a pleating effect results, allowing the accordion to lie flat and spread out.

Two accordions can be joined by the addition of a small hinge.

A further development is that of folding in incremental decreases.

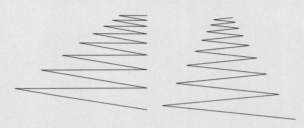

An accordion can also be constructed by joining folded sections (folios). Following are three examples from Japanese album structures, showing options for joining folios at the back edge; joining by alternating folios front to back; and joining folios at the fore-edge.

The accordion can also be employed as a spine. In these three examples individual folios are: sewn onto the mountain fold; sewn into the valley fold; and attached around a mountain fold.

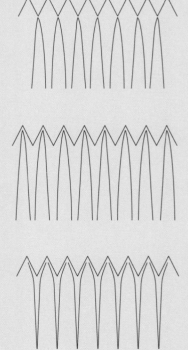

Folding in an irregular pattern, alternating one large double section and one single small section, the resulting accordion yields surprising results. We explore this further in Chapter 3, One-Sheet Books.

1 Folding an Accordion 2–4–8

This technique of folding an accordion has been taught by Hedi for many years and the idea is simple: you want to arrive at an accordion with many sections, but you don't want an incremental mistake at each fold to add up. By folding a sheet of paper in half, and then each half (and only each half) in half again, you are limiting the possibility for inaccuracy. This halving actually doubles the amount of sections each time and a phenomenon arises. A mathematician would call it an exponential increase following a geometric progression. We call it magical. With each progression, 1 section becomes 2, 2 become 4, 4 become 8, 8 become 16 and so on, doubling each time.

The method we describe here lines up mountain folds at the same edge, which we are calling the designated edge, where they can be controlled so as not to shift. The resulting valley folds line up at the opposite edge. This kind of folding has a good rhythm and can become very intuitive. With some care, you can arrive at a perfect accordion every time.

In the project following this, we describe an exponential increase of 3–6–12. Both of these methods leave out divisions of, for example, 5, 11 or 15. Our solution? Fold to one of our described progressions and then cut off the sections you don't need to arrive at your desired number. Another solution is to fold with extensions, also found in this chapter. By reserving some paper attached to but not folded with the accordion, they can be carefully matched later. Practice folding, using any kind of paper, even with the grain running in the wrong direction. It is the best way to experience the amazing characteristics of the accordion.

COMPONENT	DIMENSIONS	QTY	MATERIAL
ACCORDION	11 x 17 in. 29.7 x 42 cm/A3	1	Text-weight paper

TOOLS:
Bone folder

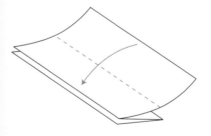

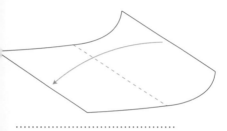

1. Fold the paper in half.

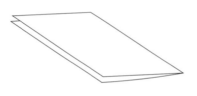

2. Crease well.

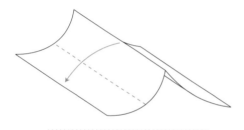

3. Open up as shown. Bring the mountain fold over, lining it up with the cut edge that will become the designated edge where all mountain folds are lined up. Crease well with the bone folder.

4. Bring the other cut edge over, lining it up with the designated edge.

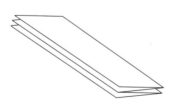

5. Crease well.

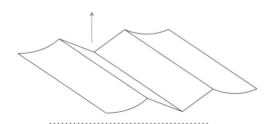

6. Open up as shown, turning the center valley fold into a mountain fold so that you now have three mountain folds.

7. Bring the first mountain fold over to the designated edge. Line up and crease well.

8. Repeat with the remaining two mountain folds, bringing them over one at a time to the designated edge and lining them up.

9. Finish with the cut edge and crease well.

10. You now have an eight-section accordion! Many projects in this book start here.

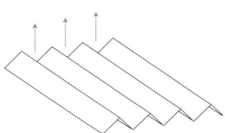

11. To create a 16-section accordion, open up as shown, turning all valley folds into mountain folds.

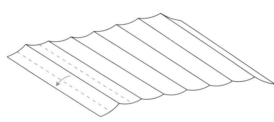

12. Bring the first mountain fold to the designated edge.

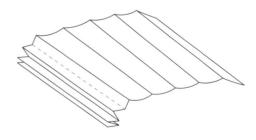

13. Repeat with the remaining six mountain folds, one at a time, lining them up and creasing well.

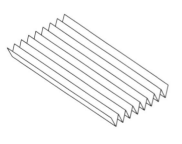

14. A 16-section accordion is very useful as a spine component in many of the structures in this book.

2 Folding an Accordion 3–6–12

We want to offer an alternative to the accordion folded in multiples of 2–4–8 and find that starting out with a paper divided into three equal parts is very helpful. For instance, you get six parts instead of four and twelve instead of eight as you keep dividing the parts you started with. This gives you options when planning your project.

COMPONENT	DIMENSIONS	QTY	MATERIAL
ACCORDION	11 x 17 in. 29.7 x 42 cm/A3	1	Text-weight paper

TOOLS:
Bone folder

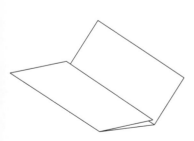

1. Divide the paper into three equal parts, making a pencil mark at one third.

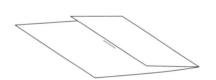

2. Bring the right edge over to the pencil mark. Crease well with your bone folder.

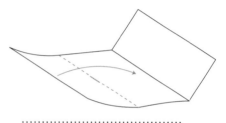

3. Open up as shown. Bring the left edge over to the resulting fold.

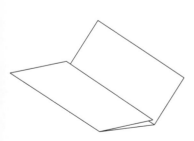

4. Crease well with your bone folder.

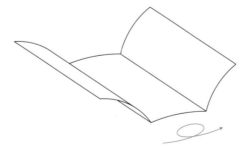

5. Open up as shown. You now have two valley folds. Turn the sheet over so that you have two mountain folds.

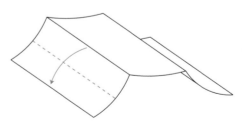

6. Bring the first mountain fold over to the cut edge that will become the designated edge where all mountain folds are lined up.

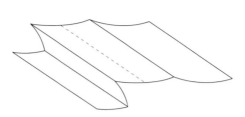

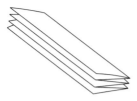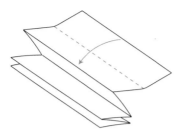

7. Crease well with the bone folder. Repeat with the remaining mountain fold...

8. ...and the cut edge, bringing them over one at a time to the designated edge, lining them up and creasing well.

9. You now have a six-section accordion. Many projects in this book start here.

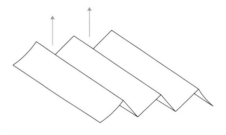

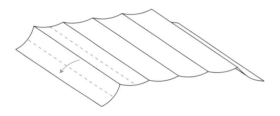

10. Open the accordion up as shown, turning all valley folds into mountain folds.

11. Bring the first mountain fold over to the designated edge, lining it up and creasing well.

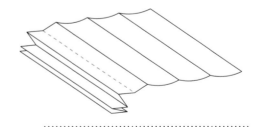

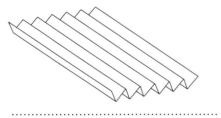

12. Repeat with the remaining mountain folds, one at a time.

13. You now have a 12-section accordion!

3 Folding an Accordion with Extensions

What do we mean by extensions? Extensions can be added to one or both sides of an accordion strip and are tucked away so as to not interfere while folding the accordion. Extensions may become hinges or even covers on small books. They are also useful to add an extra section if the divisions of your accordion do not correspond with the number of divisions you need. Extensions need to be planned in advance to become an integral part of the structure. After you have folded the accordion, carefully match the extension with the width of the accordion section and cut to size. Please read the introduction on folding an accordion on pages 28–29.

COMPONENT	DIMENSIONS	QTY	MATERIAL
ACCORDION	11 x 17 in. 29.7 x 42 cm/A3	1	Text-weight paper

TOOLS:
Bone folder

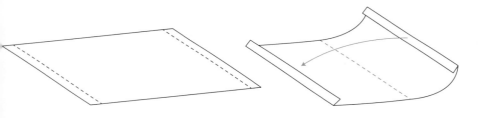

1. Mark and score a line ¾ in. (2 cm) on both sides of the paper.

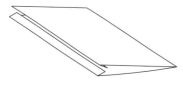

2. Fold these two extensions as shown and crease well with your bone folder.

3. Bring the right edge over to the left edge. Crease well.

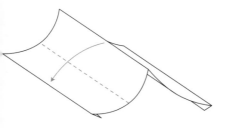

4. Open up as shown. Bring the mountain fold over to the designated edge, lining it up and creasing well.

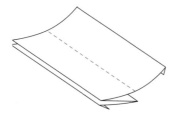

5. Finish by bringing the remaining folded edge over.

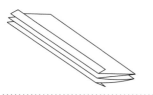

6. You now have four sections with extensions on either side.

4 Simple Accordion

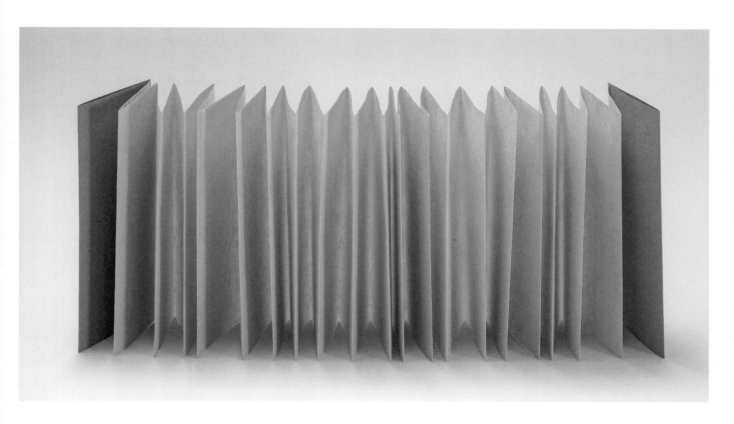

As a structure, the simple accordion is not complicated. It builds upon the project at the beginning of this chapter, Folding an Accordion 2–4–8. Utilizing five accordion sections, the result is a book that is 12 feet or close to 4 meters long! It may take careful planning, but the reward will be a book of subtle elegance and graceful movement as the pages fan back and forth. Do not underestimate the benefit of practice making perfect in the art of folding. For this project we suggest that you indulge in some beautiful Japanese paper and plan for a generous number of pages. You do not have to follow our dimensions. Nothing can go wrong. Short or tall, wide or narrow, the basic techniques described here can be easily adapted.

The simple accordion structure yields wildly different results when made out of other materials, including Tyvek, printed matter, recycled material, old office supplies, handmade paper, paper on a roll or cardstock. Experiment!

NOTE
Accuracy in folding and positioning the parts before connecting them is essential here to achieve the best result. We advise that you study the diagrams and practice folding an accordion until you feel confident and are happy with the outcome. Refer to Folding an Accordion 2–4–8, pages 30–32, and follow to step 10, using the paper dimensions given here.

COMPONENT	DIMENSIONS	QTY	MATERIAL
ACCORDION	8 x 30 in. 20 x 76 cm	5	Lightweight paper: Japanese paper (Tatami, Obonai Feather, Dai Chiri, Mulberry)
COVERS	8 x 8 in. 20 x 20 cm	2	Cardstock: Japanese linen cardstock, 244g

FINISHED DIMENSIONS:
8 x 4 in. (20 x 9.5 cm)

TOOLS:
Self-healing cutting mat / Straight edge / Sharp knife or paper cutter / Bone folder / Pencil / Scissors / Ruler / Double-sided tape

TECHNIQUES:
Folding an Accordion 2–4–8, pages 30–32

Cutting Angles, Darts and Slivers, page 21

Group A

Group B

1. Cut five strips to the exact same size and fold each strip into an eight-section accordion. Orient three of the five accordions facing right (group A) and two facing left (group B).

2. Turn the first and last sections of each accordion in group A over to the left.

3. Apply double-sided tape to the turned-over sections in group A.

4. Trim off the remaining parts of the sections just beyond the tape, leaving narrow hinges.

5. In group B, trim off slivers from the first and last sections of each accordion to achieve a better fit when joining.

6. Loosely organize group A accordions together with group B accordions, as shown.

7. Study the zig-zag diagram to understand how the three hinged accordions and the two non-hinged accordions will be positioned before connecting.

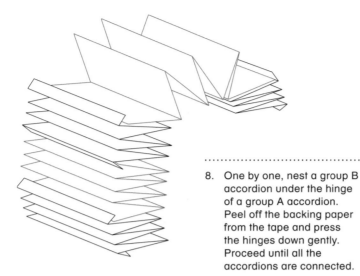

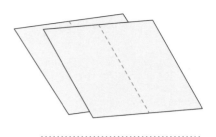

8. One by one, nest a group B accordion under the hinge of a group A accordion. Peel off the backing paper from the tape and press the hinges down gently. Proceed until all the accordions are connected.

9. Cut your covers to size.

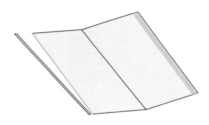

10. Fold each one in half.

11. Trim off 1/16 in. (2 mm) from one of the long sides of each cover and apply double-sided tape to the opposite edge.

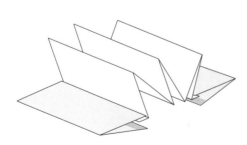

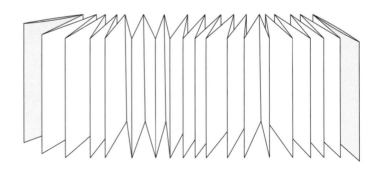

12. Take each cover in turn and position and attach it underneath the front and back hinges. Only one of the five accordions is shown here for clarity.

13. Peel off the backing paper from the tape on the hinges and adhere to the accordion, as shown.

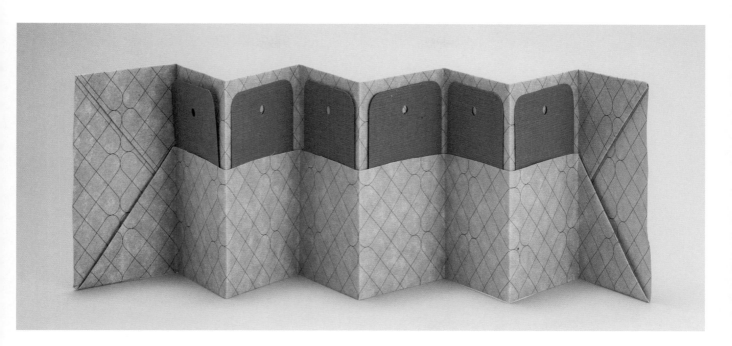

A little wonder, this accordion pocket employs simple geometry to yield any number of outcomes. We describe three variations in this chapter but, depending on the paper size you choose to experiment with, you will discover endless possibilities. As with many projects in this book, the techniques learned here (the cover of this structure, for example), can be adapted to other structures. Accordion pockets help you organize random items such as stamps, receipts, tickets or business cards. Filled with ephemera, photographs, swatches and scraps, they also make unusual gifts.

NOTE

Proportions are important here, as their relationship is the foundation of this structure. The paper is twice as wide as it is high. Cutting off a small portion from the height allows the lower and upper rows of squares to overlap and thus create the pockets.

COMPONENT	DIMENSIONS	QTY	MATERIAL
ACCORDION	8¼ x 17 in. 20 x 42 cm	1	Text-weight paper: French Speckletone 70T
COVERS	3⅞ x 8½ in. 9.5 x 21 cm	1	Cardstock: Japanese linen cardstock, 244g
INSERTS	3½ x 1¾ in. 8.5 x 4.5 cm	6	Cardstock: Japanese linen cardstock, 244g

FINISHED DIMENSIONS:
3⅞ x 2⅛ in. (9.5 x 5.2 cm)

TOOLS:
Self-healing cutting mat / Straight edge / Sharp knife or paper cutter / Bone folder / Pencil / Ruler / Double-sided tape / Corner rounder (optional)

TECHNIQUES:
Folding an Accordion 2–4–8, pages 30–32

Scaling Proportions Up or Down, page 18

Making Non-Tear Slits with Anchor Holes, page 21

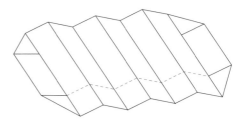

1. Fold an eight-section accordion. Fold the upper and lower corners of the first and last sections diagonally inward to the first and last valley folds.

2. Fold the bottom edge upward, establishing the fold along the base of the triangles. When making long folds such as this, matching vertical folds ensures accurate results.

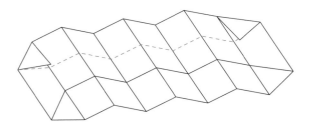

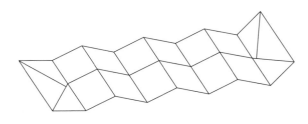

3. Fold the top edge down toward the middle, creating a small overlap.

4. Tuck the top edge under the bottom edge.

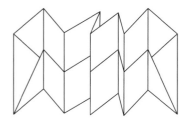

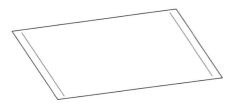

5. Refold the accordion, starting at the middle mountain fold.

6. Prepare the cover. Confirm that the height of the cover is the exact height of your folded pocket accordion. Trim or cut the cover slightly larger if necessary. Draw pencil lines 5/16 in. (8 mm) away from the short edges.

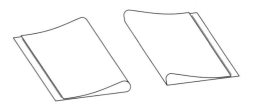

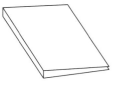

7. Bring the right short edge to the left pencil line and crease well. Repeat with the left edge.

8. This will establish a folded spine exactly in the middle of the cover piece.

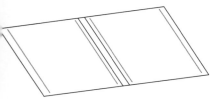

9. Open the cover and draw pencil lines on both sides of the spine ¼ in. (6 mm) away.

10. Fold the right and left edges inward to meet those lines and crease well.

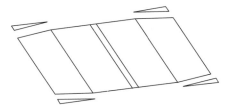

11. Cut off narrow angles at the corners of the cover, as shown.

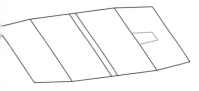

12. Mark and cut a tab at the back of the inner cover. We centered and tapered the tab as shown. Feel free to come up with your own version.

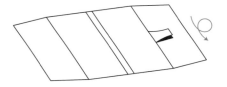

13. Turn the cover over.

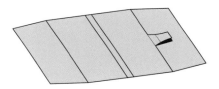

14. Score the tab ⁵⁄₁₆ in. (8 mm) away from the fore-edge fold.

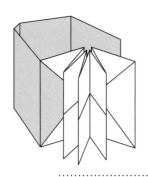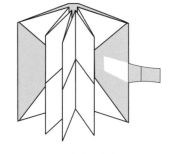

15. Insert the cover into the pockets. It should fit snugly and the cover should match the height of the structure.

16. Wrap the tab around to the front cover and mark for a slit the tab can slip into. To cut this slit, take the front cover out of the pocket and make the cut on a mat. Reassemble and fill with the inserts.

A deceptively simple project, this is a variation of the Pocket Accordion with Separate Cover. Instead of cutting the paper to calculated proportions, we used uncut standard sheets. If you look at the diagram of the finished structure, you'll see that the triangles at the inside front and back covers no longer start at the corners. There is no math involved here. Different sizes of paper will work, as long as they have roughly the same proportions as standard sheets (11 x 17 in. / A3).

COMPONENT	DIMENSIONS	QTY	MATERIAL
ACCORDION	11 x 17 in. 29.7 x 42 cm/A3	1	Text-weight paper: French Speckletone 70T
INSERTS	4¾ x 1¾ in. 12 x 4.5 cm	6	Cover-weight paper or cardstock: Japanese linen cardstock, 244g

TECHNIQUE:
Folding an Accordion 2–4–8, pages 30–32

FINISHED DIMENSIONS:
5¼ x 2⅛ in. from an
11 x 17-in. sheet
(14 x 5.2 cm from an A3 sheet)

TOOLS:
Self-healing cutting mat / Straight edge / Sharp knife or paper cutter / Bone folder / Pencil / Ruler / Corner rounder (optional)

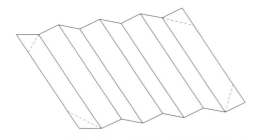

1. Fold an eight-section accordion. Open as shown.

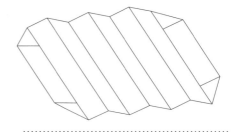

2. Fold the corners of the first and last sections diagonally inward to the first and last valley folds.

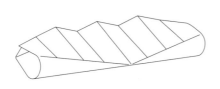

3. Bend the paper in half (do not fold) and make a small crease mark with your thumb at the middle of the vertical center fold.

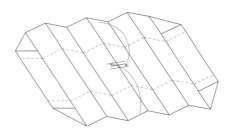

4. Make two pencil lines ¼ in. (5 mm) above and below the crease mark. Fold the bottom edge to the upper pencil mark and the upper edge to the lower pencil mark. This will create an overlap of ½ in. (1 cm).

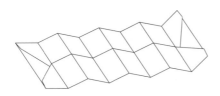

5. Tuck the top edge underneath the bottom edge.

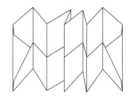

6. Refold the accordion, starting at the middle mountain fold. Fill the pocket accordion with contents of your choosing.

This four-pocket accordion with double covers and a spine is unique in that it accomplishes all this from a single sheet of paper. A new technique learned here is that of adding extensions to the accordion, reserved for use as a spine. A bit more complex than the previous pocket accordion, this model explores the wonder of making a book from a single sheet of paper.

The three variations of Pocket Accordion presented in this chapter are shown in the photo above. They comprise a family of structures that can be manipulated individually or combined into a series, perhaps given a slipcase to contain them (pages 176–83).

NOTE:

Throughout this book, we present measurements in both imperial and metric units. They are not exact conversions of each other – one done using inches may produce results of slightly different dimensions than one using centimeters. However, in each system of measurement the proportion of the structure is maintained.

COMPONENT	DIMENSIONS	QTY	MATERIAL
ACCORDION	7 x 17 in.(18 x 42 cm), including 2 in. (4 cm) for extensions	I	Text-weight paper: French Speckletone 70T
INSERTS	3¼ x 1¾ in. 8.5 x 4.5 cm	6	Cover-weight paper or cardstock: Japanese linen cardstock, 244g

FINISHED DIMENSIONS:
3¼ x 1⅞ in. (8.5 x 5 cm)

TOOLS:
Self-healing cutting mat / Straight edge / Sharp knife or paper cutter / Bone folder / Pencil / Ruler / Corner rounder (optional) / Glue

TECHNIQUES:
Folding an Accordion with Extensions, pages 35–39

Inside Reverse Fold, page 22

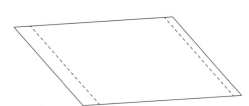

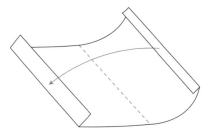

1. Mark and score a line 1¼ in. (or 2.5 cm) from the left side and a line ¾ in. (or 1.5 cm) from the right side of the accordion strip. These mark the extensions for the spine.

2. Fold the extensions and crease well. These will not be folded as part of the accordion.

3. Fold the remaining portion into an eight-section accordion.

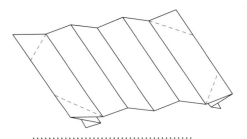

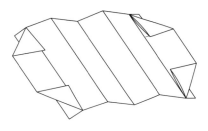

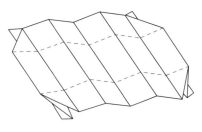

4. Open the accordion. With the 1¼-in. (2.5-cm) extension to the left, fold the extension and first section under. Repeat on the right side.

5. Pick up the first double section on the left side and fold the lower and upper corners diagonally to the first valley fold. Repeat on the right side so that all four corners are folded inward.

6. Inside reverse fold all four triangles by opening them up and pushing them inward.

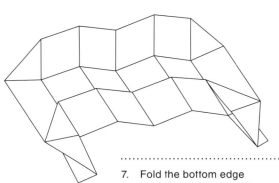

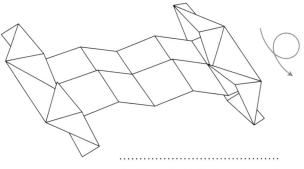

7. Fold the bottom edge upward, establishing the fold along the base of the triangles. When making long folds such as this, matching vertical folds ensures accurate results.

8. Repeat with the top edge and tuck it underneath the bottom edge. Turn the strip over.

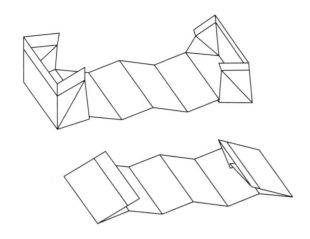

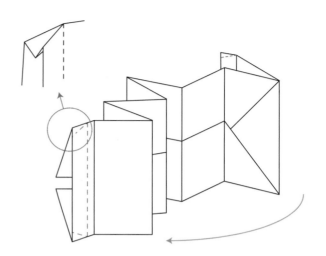

9. Inside reverse fold the four corner triangles and the extensions so that the first and last sections lie flat.

10. Make a ¼-in. (or 7-mm) spine fold on the wider extension. Make a diagonal fold and then inside reverse fold the corners of the extension in preparation for the next step. Rotate as shown.

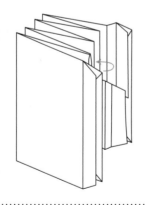

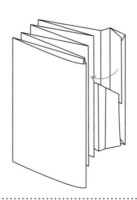

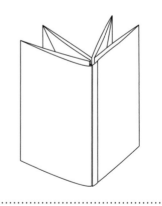

11. Insert the narrower extension into the pocket adjacent to it.

12. Insert the remaining larger extension into the same pocket. Use a little glue to secure the spine in place.

13. Fill the pocket accordion with contents of your choosing. We rounded the corners and punched holes in our inserts.

8 Pop-Up Accordion

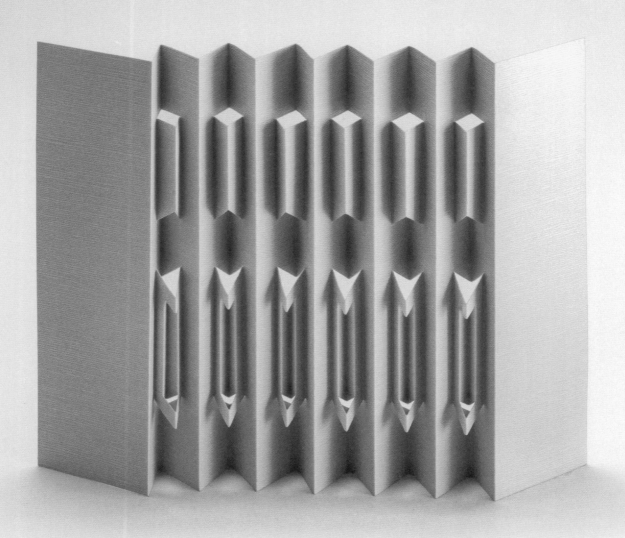

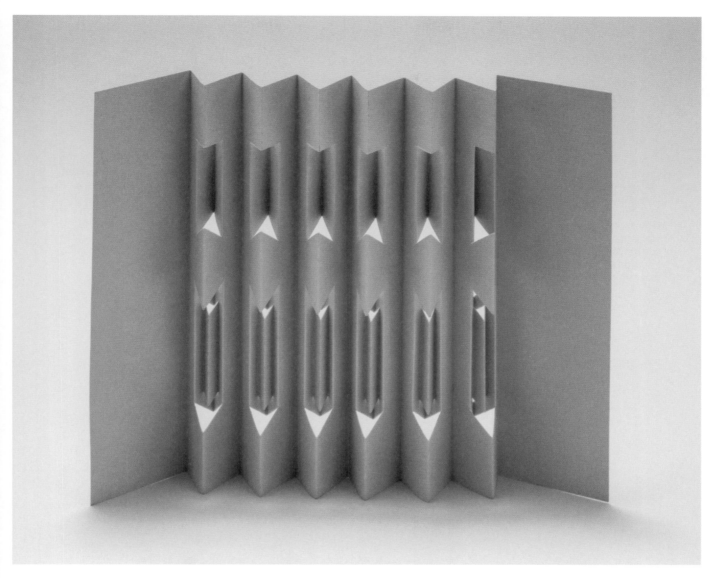

Here we present a simple example of a pop-up accordion. Pop-ups have a special place in the book world. Engineered to surprise, they are always ingenious and sometimes unbelievable. The accordion fold is an ideal medium for the display of identical pop-ups, as the repetition evokes architectural spaces. This project could hardly be more minimal – four cuts, two folds and a bit of pushing in is all it takes. Once you have made and understand the mechanics of this one, you can explore endless permutations.

NOTE
To make successful pop-ups, it's a very good idea to experiment first. We provide the shapes for this project as an introduction to this technique. To design your own shape, cut a scrap of paper to the width of one section of the accordion and establish a vertical center line. Take care not to let the shape extend beyond this center line – otherwise, as they fold in and out, they will extend beyond the confines of the page.

COMPONENT	DIMENSIONS	QTY	MATERIAL
ACCORDION	8 x 20 in. 20 x 48 cm	1	Cover-weight paper: Elephant hide paper, 190 gsm
TEMPLATE	8 x 1¼ in. 20 x 3 cm	1	Cardstock

FINISHED DIMENSIONS:
8 x 2½ in. (20 x 6 cm)

TOOLS:
Self-healing cutting mat / Straight edge / Sharp knife or paper cutter / Bone folder / Pencil / Ruler / Awl

TECHNIQUES:
Folding an Accordion 2–4–8, pages 30–32

Measuring Devices: Templates, page 19

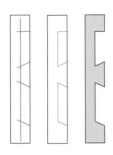

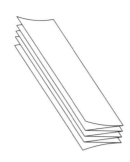

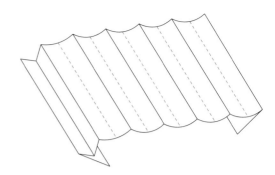

1. Prepare the template by drawing a center line lengthwise on the strip of cardstock. Draw one short horizontal line and three diagonal lines from one edge to the middle. Make cuts as shown in the diagram. Set aside.

2. Fold the accordion strip into eight sections.

3. Open the accordion and fold the first and last sections under to reserve for the front and back covers. Reverse valley folds into mountain folds and fold the six remaining sections into 12 sections.

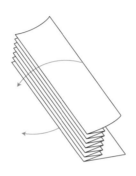

4. Collapse the accordion. Flip the reserved sections (covers) to the left.

5. You should have six mountain folds (12 sections), with the folded edge facing to the right. Place the template on top of the 12 sections. With an awl, pierce holes marking the four corners of each cut-out on the template.

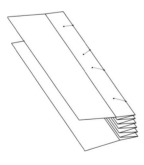

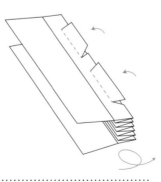

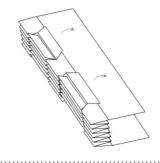

6. Cut through all 12 layers from the inner marks to the outer marks.

7. Do not make any vertical cuts. If the stack is too thick, divide it in half and repeat this step. Tabs are created where you've made the cuts. Lift the tabs as shown, folding them over to the left and creasing the folds with your bone folder. Repeat until all tabs are folded in the same direction.

8. Turn the stack over and fold the tabs in the opposite direction.

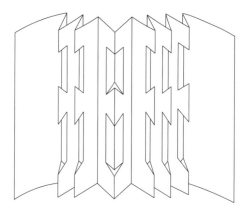

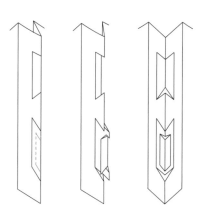

9. Open the accordion.
   Push the tabs inward.

10. In our model, we've cut a third tab within the lower tab. Experiment with this method. It requires two additional cuts and the resulting tab gets pushed forward for a more three-dimensional effect.

VARIATION
Using a gouge for woodworking, experiment by punching out shapes that play with light and shadow.

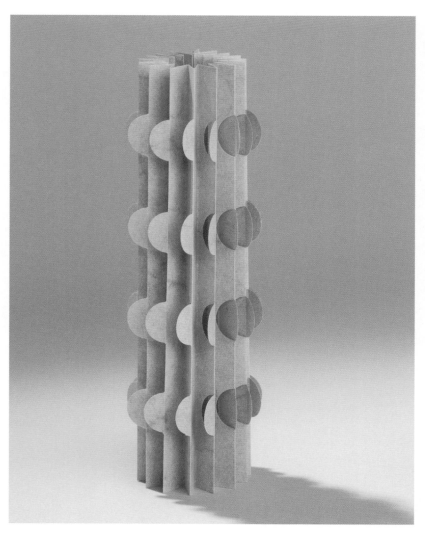

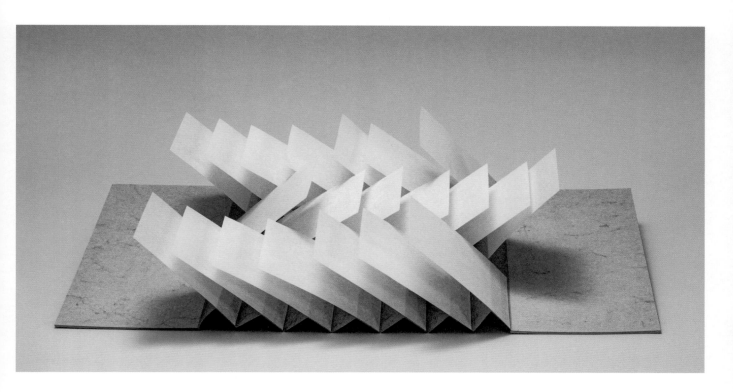

The Flag Book may be described as a portable, expandable file that can display an array of materials in an animated way. Operating with the assistance of the accordion fold, it has the freedom to expand and retract. It can be read page by page or pulled apart for the full effect of an uninterrupted scenario. Standing, the Flag Book also will turn into a circular or star book as the covers are held together at the back. A fascinating view reveals itself when the spine sides of the covers are brought forward and joined to create a flat surface while the pages curve into spirals.

Known as a noisemaker when the flags are shaken back and forth, the Flag Book was one of the pioneering structures that opened up a new field for book artists. It was engineered with the idea in mind to capture "bookness" without traditional limits. The structure allows for boundless variations and has been adapted to many uses – we encourage you to experiment. The given measurements need not be followed, nor do you have to adhere to the number of flags, their size or their shape. Content can be added after the book is done. You may also cut a print or photograph into the three flag strips. Be aware that the middle row of flags goes in the opposite direction. Should you decide to use text or an image that needs to be oriented in a certain way, it's very important to explore with a model first.

This Flag Book has covers that are more time consuming to make and require some drying time while weighted down. We recommend you give it a try. You can make these covers for other projects as well. Hard covers are more substantial and they have a nice finished look.

COMPONENT	DIMENSIONS	QTY	MATERIAL
ACCORDION	8 x 13 in. 20 x 33 cm	1	Text-weight paper: Elephant hide paper 110 gsm
COVER BOARDS	8 x 4 in. 20 x 10 cm	2	Board: Davey board .060
COVER PAPERS	9½ x 5½ in. 23 x 13 cm	2	Text-weight paper: Elephant hide paper 110 gsm with printed pattern
BOARD SHEETS	7⅝ x 3⅝ in. 19 x 9 cm	2	
FLAG STRIPS	17½ x 3¾ in. (45.5 x 10 cm) yields 7 flags each	3	Cover Weight Paper: Vegetable parchment

FINISHED DIMENSIONS:
8 x 4 in. (20 x 10 cm)

TOOLS:
Self-healing cutting mat / Straight edge / Sharp knife or paper cutter / Bone folder / Pencil / Scissors / Ruler / Glue brush / Pressing boards / Weights / Double-sided tape / Mixture (adhesive)

TECHNIQUES:
Folding an Accordion 2–4–8, pages 30–32

Use of Adhesive when Preparing Stiff Covers, page 25

Dividing into an Odd Number of Sections, page 20

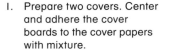

1. Prepare two covers. Center and adhere the cover boards to the cover papers with mixture.

2. Trim the corners at 45-degree angles, leaving 1½ times the thickness of the board between the corner and the cut.

3. Starting at the head and tail, bring the turn-ins onto the board. Use your thumbnail (or bone folder) to pinch the extra paper at the corners against the board's edges.

4. Bring the remaining turn-ins at the spine and fore-edge onto the board; you may need to add more mixture before you do this. Smooth and flatten with your bone folder. Place under weighted boards for several hours.

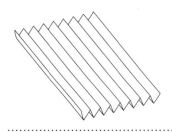

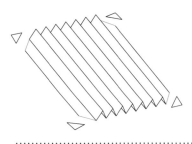

5. Meanwhile, fold the accordion strip into 16 sections.

6. Open the accordion. The first and last sections will be the hinges. Cut off small triangles at the four corners of the hinges. This will prevent the hinges from showing at the head and tail after the covers are attached.

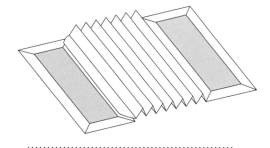

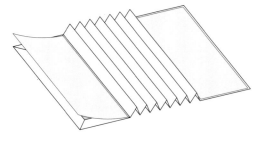

7. Retrieve the covers and attach them to the back and front accordion hinges with mixture. Place under weights and let dry.

8. Apply mixture to the board sheets and paste them to the inside of the covers, hiding the hinges and leaving an even space all around. Lay the covers out flat to either side of the accordion and let them dry under weighted boards for at least one hour – or preferably overnight.

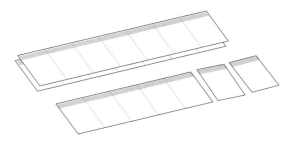

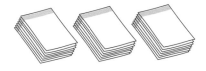

9. Prepare the flag strips by attaching double-sided tape to the reverse side of each strip (lengthwise), then mark and cut each strip into seven equal parts.

10. Arrange the flags in three piles of seven flags each.

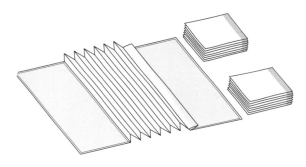

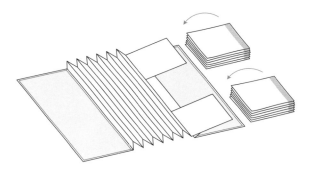

11. Open the accordion and position two stacks of flags next to the back cover. Starting at the back of the book, fold the first double section of the accordion down to the right.

12. Take a flag from each stack, peel off the backing paper from the tape and carefully press to adhere the flags to the double section. One flag is placed flush at the head and the other one flush at the tail.

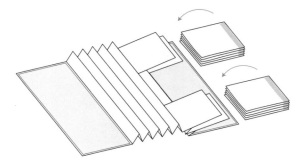

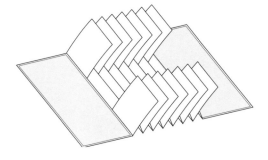

13. Fold the next double section of the accordion down to the right. Peel off the backing paper from the tape from two more flags, lining them up with the ones below, and attach.

14. Continue until all 14 flags are in place. You are now at the front of the book.

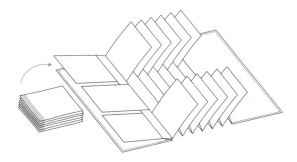

15. Take the third stack of flags and position next to the front cover. Turn the first double section of the accordion down to your left. Peel off the backing paper from the tape from one flag and adhere it, centering it between the other two.

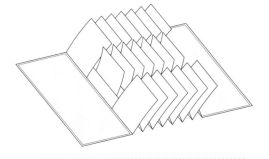

16. Continue with the remaining six flags to the end of the row.

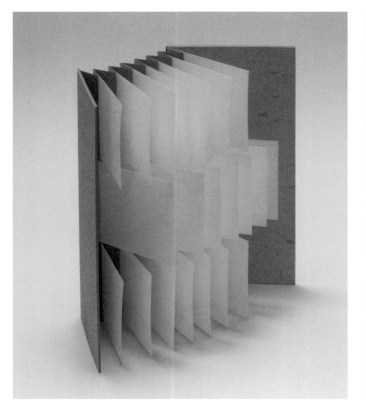

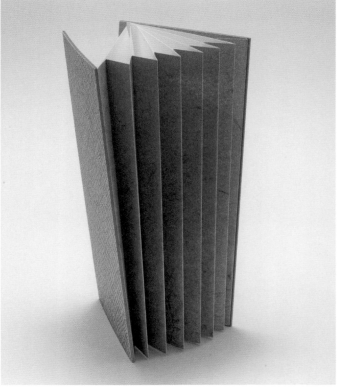

This structure is a variation of the previous project in this chapter, the Flag Book. It has a single accordion spine with flags on either side. The size of the flags varies – some tall, some short. The flags can be found paper ephemera such as postcards, photos, tickets, stamps, etc. We improvised with the covers, using a dense press-board that is recycled from old file folders, comes in a variety of colors and requires no further covering. The process of attaching the flags is similar to that described in the previous project, omitting the bottom row.

The beauty of this variation of the Flag Book is that there is no front or back, top or bottom until you decide on content. In this model we set one double row of flags flush with the edge of the accordion and one double row slightly inset. Note that there are six flags on one side and seven flags on the other. This is a very versatile book structure. If you are feeling brave, why not give it a try?

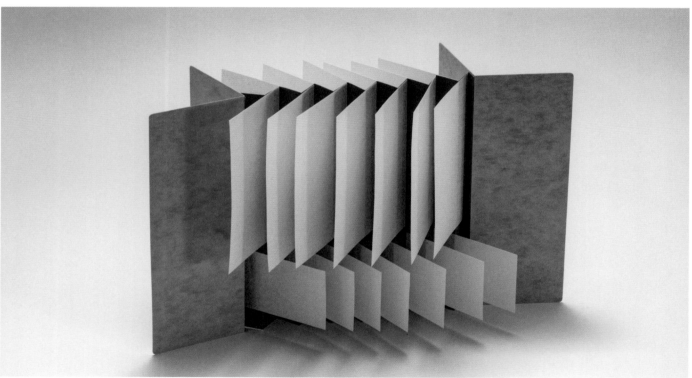

COMPONENT	DIMENSIONS	QTY	MATERIAL
ACCORDION STRIP	8 x 12 in. 20 x 31 cm	1	Text-weight paper: Recycled packaging paper
COVERS	8 x 6 in. 20 x 15 cm	2	Board: Recycled press-board
FLAGS (SMALL)	2 x 3 in. 5 x 7.5 cm	13	Cover-weight paper: Vegetable parchment
FLAGS (LARGE)	5 x 3 in. 12.5 x 7.5 cm	13	Cover-weight paper: Vegetable parchment

FINISHED DIMENSIONS:

8 x 6 in. (20 x 15 cm)

TOOLS:

Self-healing cutting mat / Straight edge / Sharp knife or paper cutter / Bone folder / Pencil / Ruler Double-sided tape

TECHNIQUE:

Folding an Accordion 2–4–8, pages 30–32

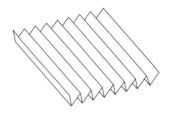

1. Fold the accordion strip into 16 sections.

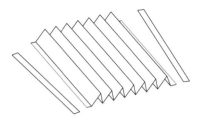

2. Open the accordion. Trim the first and last sections to ³⁄₈ in. (1 cm) wide. These will become the hinges to attach the covers.

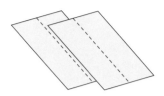

3. Prepare two covers. With a bone folder, score a line lengthwise at the midpoint on the reverse side of the covers.

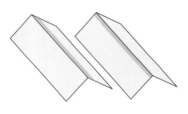

4. Fold at this score line and attach double-sided tape close to this fold.

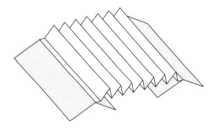

5. Attach the accordion to the covers, as shown.

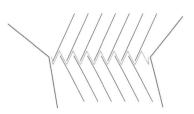

6. As in the previous project, prepare flags with double-sided tape adhered to the reverse side of each flag. Attach the smaller flags to the accordion as indicated in this diagram.

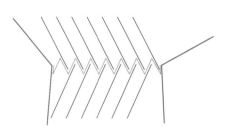

7. Attach the larger flags below, alternating their direction with the flag row above. Align the bottoms of the flags flush with the bottom of the accordion. This is necessary if you want the book to stand as a display.

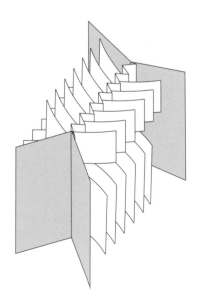

8. The beauty of this structure is its reversibility: having no strong beginning or end, front or back, it can be viewed from any direction.

11 Interlocking Loops

Interlocking Loops, a relative of the Flag Book, features flags that resemble loops. The alternating directions of the loops make it an effective and lively display for a collection of symbols, photographs or practically anything you can think of. Because of its three-dimensional structure, it stands up very well. As the loops are double sided, why not cut a window in the top layer to view images underneath? Why not shape the loops themselves or increase their size and number? A particular curiosity presents itself as the covers are pulled apart and the loops are stretched out flat, barely recognizable. Upon bringing the covers close together with a wriggling, shaking motion, the loops re-establish themselves thanks to the memory of the fold.

COMPONENT	DIMENSIONS	QTY	MATERIAL
ACCORDION	8 x 22½ in. 20 x 60 cm	1	Text-weight paper: Elephant hide paper, 110 gsm
COVERS	8 x 8 in. 20 x 20 cm	2	Cover-weight paper or cardstock: Japanese linen cardstock, 244g Handmade Zaansch bord

FINISHED DIMENSIONS:

8 x 4 in. (20 x 10.5 cm)

TOOLS:

Self-healing cutting mat / Straight edge / Sharp knife or paper cutter Bone folder / Pencil / Ruler / Awl Double-sided tape

TECHNIQUES:

Folding an Accordion 3–6–12, pages 33–34

Dividing into an Odd Number of Sections, page 20

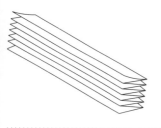

1. Fold the accordion strip into 12 sections.

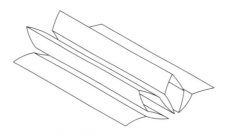

2. Refold it into six sections, using the existing folds.

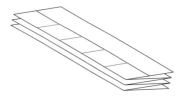

3. Divide the center fold line on the top section into five equal parts. Lightly draw four perpendicular lines from the center fold to the left fore-edge.

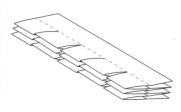

4. Cut along these four pencil lines through all six layers. Start the cuts at the fold rather than at the fore-edge.

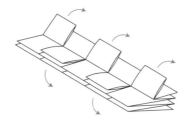

5. Fold the first, third and fifth loops of the first double section to your right and crease well.

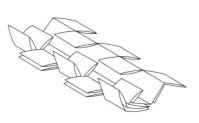

6. Turn that double section over and fold the second and fourth loops to your left.

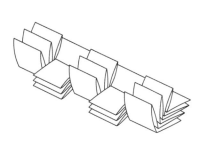

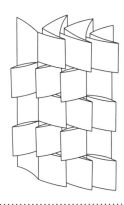

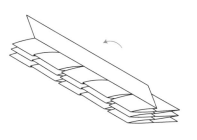

7. Repeat steps 5 and 6 with the remaining two double sections.

8. Gently pull the accordion apart and crease the loops one by one in the directions indicated.

9. Collapse the structure and bring the first single section over to the left, exposing the reverse side.

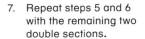

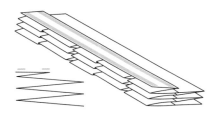

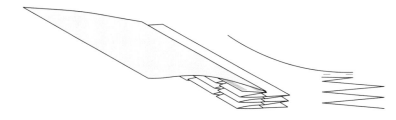

10. Apply two strips of double-sided tape, as shown. Peel away the backing paper from the inner strip.

11. Retrieve your covers and position one on top of the exposed tape. Press down. Gently lift the free side of the cover and remove the backing paper from the other strip of tape underneath. Press the cover down.

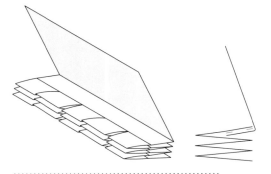

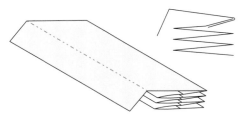

12. Bring the cover to the right and score with a bone folder along the edge of the section. Fold the cover over to the left along the score line.

13. The cover is now too wide and needs one more fold. Lay the cover down, and score with a bone folder, 4 in. (10.5 cm) from the fold created in the previous step. Make this a mountain fold.

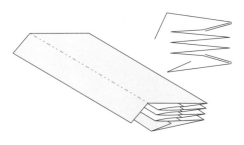

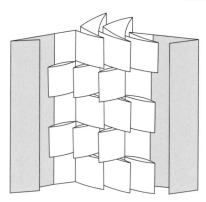

14. Repeat steps 9 through 13 to attach the back cover.

15. Pull the accordion open. Coax the loops into alternating directions, as shown. The better the creases, the better the loops will fall into position. This structure is ideal as a standing display.

The addition of printed or drawn content can easily enliven this structure and turn it into a portable gallery.

2
Blizzards

Blizzards

The gift of an unexpected day off from work due to a blizzard was put to use by embarking on an intense folding session. As the day faded away, a form emerged and was named in honor of the blizzard. Many years later, there is now a Blizzard clan. The original blizzard book and its relatives are, for the first time, all united in this chapter.

A unique characteristic of this family of folded structures is the fact that they bind themselves. All blizzards start out as accordions; through a series of diagonal folds, triangles become the mechanism that both locks the pages together at the spine and holds the content. Neither sewing nor adhesives are required in any of the blizzard variations.

Blizzard proportions are an integral part of their identity and the initial layout of a blizzard is a necessary part of the exercise. We begin with a unit square that represents the width of the blizzard we want to make. This square is placed at the top and bottom of a rectangle and, when folded, will become our triangle. The crucial part to consider for a specific model is the zone in between the two squares. When this is less than the height of the unit square, triangles will overlap. As it gets higher than the unit square, the triangles move apart. The Blizzard Book and the Wheel of Fortune have a finite range, while the Blizzard Box and the Crown Book have minimum sizes but no maximum – they can extend literally to infinity.

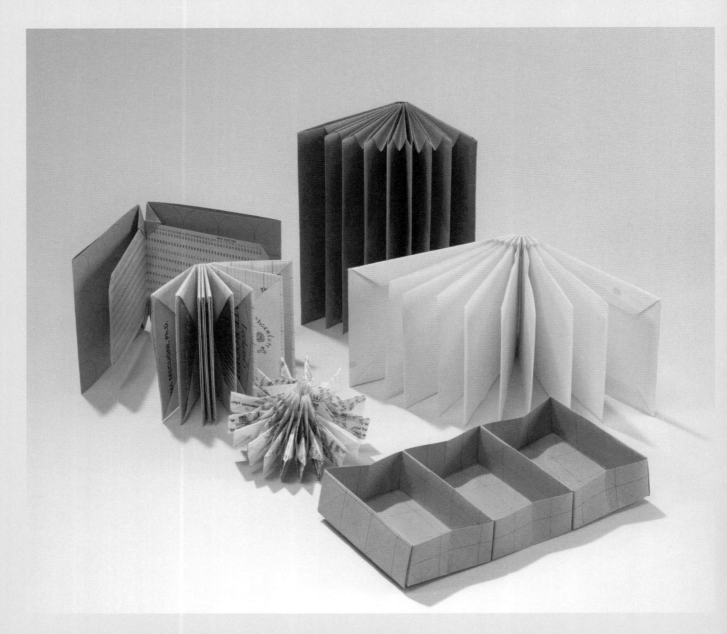

In the charts below we compare the arrangement of layout options characteristic for each of the models, showing the range in which each blizzard performs best. Once the layout panel is established, simply multiply by the number of sections in the accordion – for instance, by four or eight or sixteen, etc. Of course, there is no limit to how long you can make a blizzard!

The outlier is the Blizzard Pocket, the layout of which is based on a rectangle rather than a square. We use a rectangle measuring three-quarters of the height of a square. For this reason, the Blizzard Pocket has its own diagram. The folding sequence is similar to that of the Blizzard Book, but the outcome is extraordinarily different. Three example layouts are presented in the diagrams, though other dimensions are possible. There is no restriction to increasing the zone between the two rectangles.

BLIZZARD PROPORTIONS

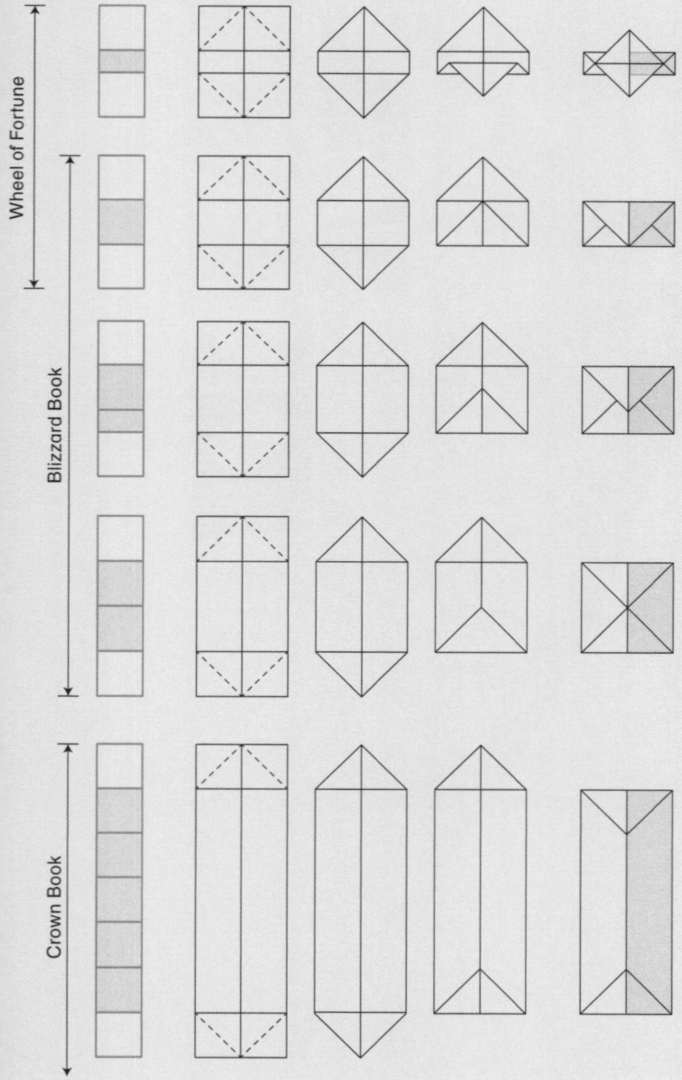

BLIZZARD POCKET PROPORTIONS

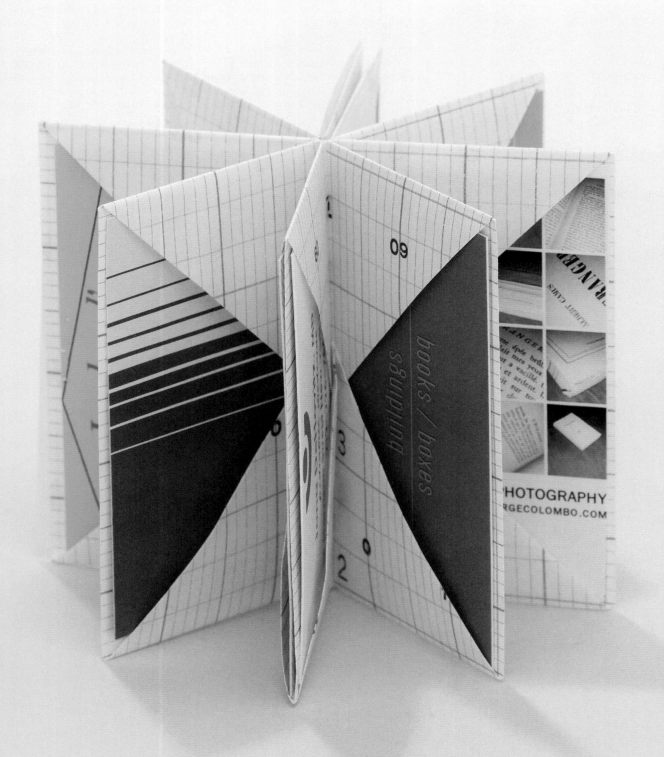

Being the progenitor from which all the members of the Blizzard clan are descended, the Blizzard Book is actually a modest compact companion, a collector, a vade mecum. As a receptacle, it can elevate the status of everyday ephemera, tags, tickets or business cards. Having been taught in workshops and courses for over 20 years, it has amassed a large following, a testament to its versatility and adaptability.

The Blizzard Book works within a proportional system in which a single section of the accordion is between three and four squares high. To see its range, refer to the diagram in the introduction to this chapter. Outside of this range, the triangles do not cooperate, overlapping either too much or not at all. This is where the Blizzard Book becomes one of the other variations in this chapter.

NOTE

This project is sized for a business card (2 x 3½ in. / 5.5 cm x 8.5 cm) as a starting point and we show two cover options.

COMPONENT	DIMENSIONS	QTY	MATERIAL
ACCORDION	7⅝ x 33 in. / 20 x 90 cm	1	Text-weight paper on a roll

TOOLS:
Self-healing cutting mat / Straight edge / Ruler / Sharp knife / Bone folder

FINISHED DIMENSIONS:
2 x 3⅝ in. (5.7 x 9 cm)

TECHNIQUES:
Folding an Accordion 2–4–8, pages 30–32

Inside Reverse Fold, page 22

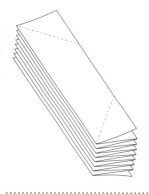

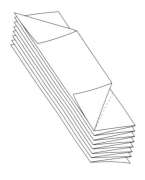

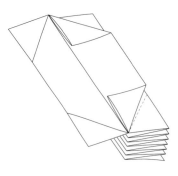

1. Fold a 16-section accordion. The open side should be facing to the right.

2. Fold right-angle triangles at the top and bottom of the first single section and crease well.

3. Unfold and turn the section to the left. Fold triangles at the next double section, taking care to line up the triangles with the vertical folds for accuracy.

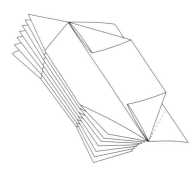

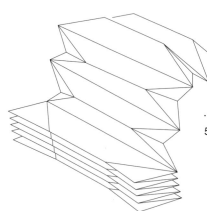

4. Unfold and turn the section to the left. Repeat with the remaining six double sections and the last single section, folding, unfolding and turning to the left.

5. Create inside reverse folds with each triangle by separating the two layers of paper and pushing the tip of the triangle (a mountain fold) into the gap created.

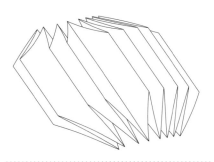

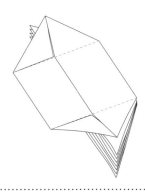

6. Complete the inside reverse folding of all triangular folds.

7. Gather up the sections. Open the first single section to the left and fold toward the center of the upper and lower tips of the triangles, taking care to align the tips with the center fold.

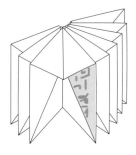

8. Turn the section to the left and repeat until all the triangles are folded in toward the center.

9. In our example the tips will overlap, making this blizzard ideal for holding cards. Depending on the proportions of your accordion, the tips may or may not overlap.

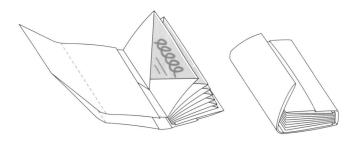

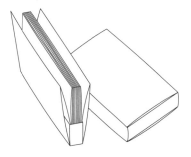

10. As a cover option for this blizzard, we used the School-Book Wrapper with Pleat (pages 172–75). The cover wraps around the book, helping to keep the contents within.

11. Another cover option is the two-part Slipcase, which we have sized for this project (see pages 176–83).

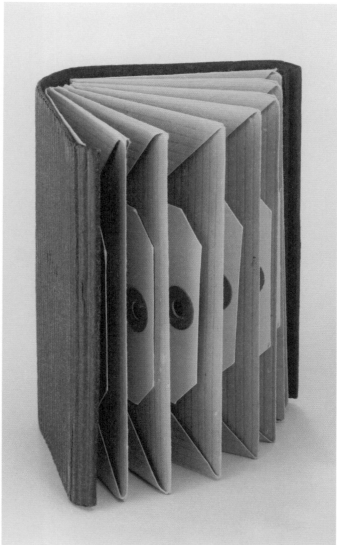

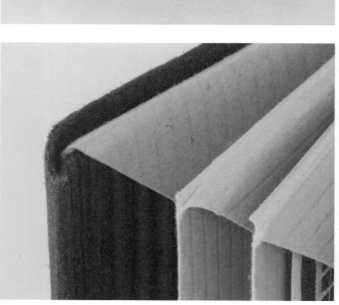

13 Wheel of Fortune

The Wheel of Fortune was a coincidental discovery, the result of not following our own rules – namely that the middle space, the zone between the two unit squares, has to be at least one square high. It is true that what results doesn't really function as a book, but we find it to be a whimsical toy that rolls and twirls.

COMPONENT	DIMENSIONS	QTY	PAPER
ACCORDION	3¾ x 24 in. 10 x 60 cm	2	Lightweight or text-weight paper on a roll

FINISHED DIMENSIONS:
2 x 3 in. (5.5 x 8 cm)

TOOLS:
Self-healing cutting mat / Straight edge / Ruler / Sharp knife / Bone folder / Double-sided tape / Awl

TECHNIQUES:
Folding an Accordion 2–4–8, pages 30–32

Inside Reverse Fold, page 22

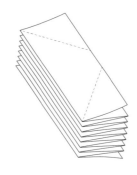

1. Fold a 16-section accordion from one of the two strips. The open side should be facing to the right. Set aside the other strip for a second wheel.

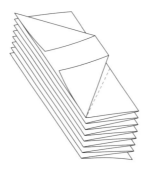

2. Fold right-angle triangles at the head and tail of the first single section.

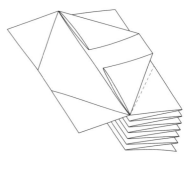

3. Crease well, unfold and turn the section to the left. Fold triangles at the next double section, taking care to line up the triangles with the vertical folds for accuracy.

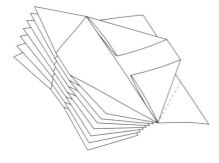

4. Unfold and turn the section to the left. Repeat with the remaining six double sections and the last single section, folding, unfolding and turning to the left.

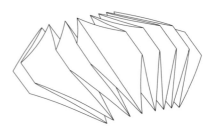

5. Inside reverse fold all the triangles (see Blizzard Book step 5, page 71).

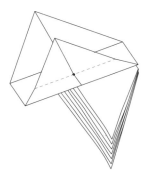

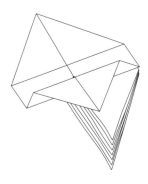

6. Gather up the sections. Open the first single section to the left and fold the tip of the lower triangle along the center fold. Mark the center of the rectangle below with an awl, piercing through all sections.

7. At the awl mark, fold the lower triangle back on itself and turn this double section to the left.

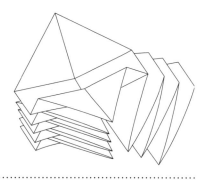

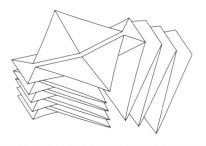

8. Repeat with all the sections, folding the lower triangles up and back.

9. When you come to the end, turn the stack around and repeat steps 6, 7 and 8 with the other triangle, turning the double sections to the left. When you come to the end of the stack, your Wheel of Fortune is complete.

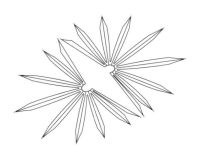

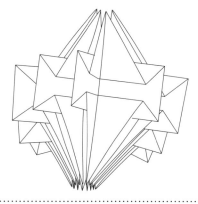

10. For a more voluminous wheel, repeat steps 1 through 9 with the remaining strip of paper. Nestle the two wheels together and attach at the single-layer "spokes" with a bit of double-sided tape.

11. This object has the potential to be made in a variety of proportions by increasing the height of the sheet of paper ever so slightly. As the photos show, wheels of different proportions play nicely with each other!

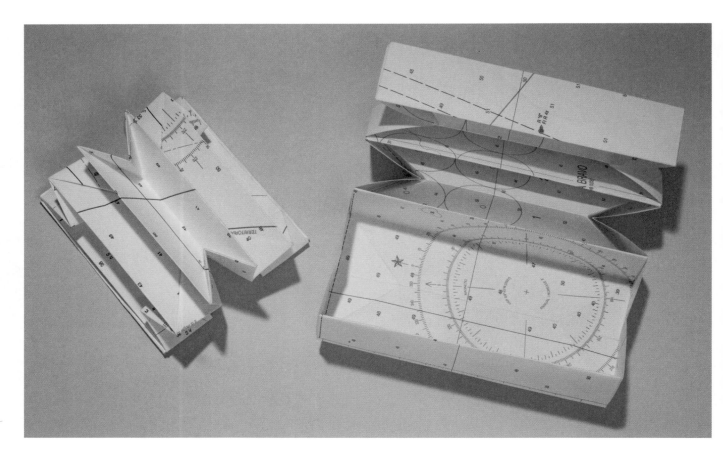

The Blizzard Box has something that none of the other members of the Blizzard clan can claim: it is collapsible. Always ready to travel, it is easily deployable, becoming a catchall and keeping track of small items. Try to stack several boxes of different heights to create more compartments, receptacles for small collections. The evolution of the Blizzard Box was the result of a spirited collaboration with a former student, Bill Hanscom. He was the first to draw up instructions for this model, which proved very helpful in developing our own.

COMPONENT	DIMENSIONS	QTY	PAPER
ACCORDION	6 x 17 in. 15 x 44 cm	1	Text-weight paper: French Dur-O-Tone 70T

FINISHED DIMENSIONS:
6½ x 4 x 1 in. (16.5 x 9 x 3 cm)

TOOLS:
Self-healing cutting mat / Straight edge
Ruler / Sharp knife / Bone folder

TECHNIQUES:
Folding an Accordion 2–4–8, pages 30–32

Inside Reverse Fold, page 22

Beginning with a unit square, use the chart below to layout boxes of different heights. Once the panel on the left is established, multiply by eight for a three-box set.

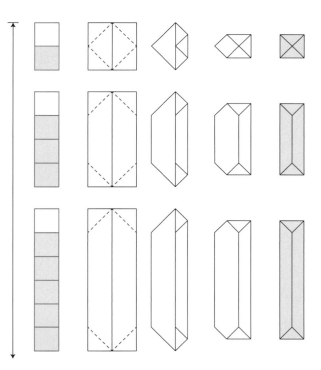

Minimum height of box is two squares, maximum height is infinite.

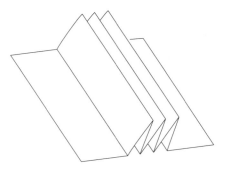

1. Fold an eight-section accordion and open the first and last single sections.

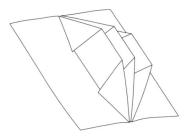

2. Fold right-angle triangles at the head and tail of the three double sections, lining up the folds with the vertical center folds.

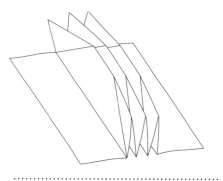

3. Crease well and unfold these triangles.

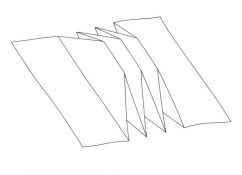

4. Inside reverse fold the triangles.

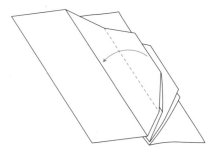

5. Gather the double sections and fold the fore-edge of the first double section to meet the center fold.

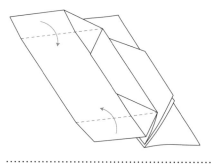

6. Bring the head and tail edges to meet the diagonal folds as shown, creating a mitered corner.

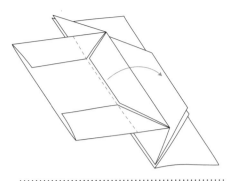

7. Unfold the fore-edge fold only and turn the double section to the left.

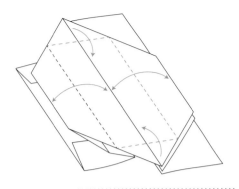

8. Make new folds as indicated by the dashed lines, the fore-edges and head and tail tips all meeting along the center fold.

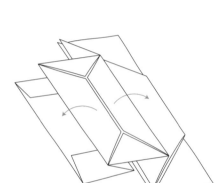

9. Unfold the right and left fore-edge folds only and turn the double section to the left. Repeat the process one more time with the third double section.

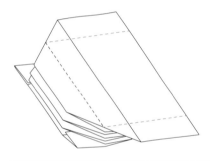

10. When you have a double section on your left and a single section on your right, bring the head and tail edges to meet the left fore-edge fold.

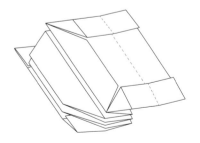

11. Fold the last fore-edge to meet the center fold.

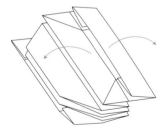

12. Unfold this last section and also the left fold.

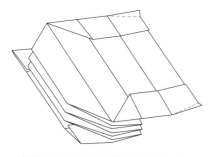

13. Make small diagonal folds at the head and tail. Inside reverse fold these triangles.

14. Bring the right edge up and over, tucking the corners into the two triangular pockets. Turn the book over and repeat steps 11 through 13 on the other side.

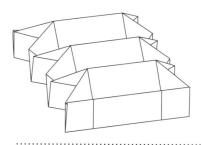

15. Gently pull the structure apart.

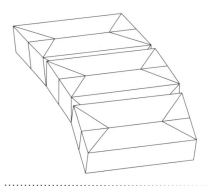

16. Pull out the sides at the head and tail and push down on the ridges until the three rectangular boxes fully emerge and snap into place. You are looking at the bottom of the boxes.

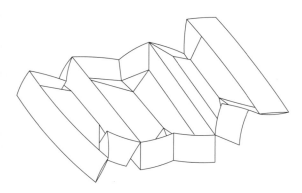

17. Turn the boxes over. Collapse the boxes into a compact rectangular packet by pushing the sides in and the bottoms up. The first time some of the folds have to be reversed from valleys into mountains, so take your time.

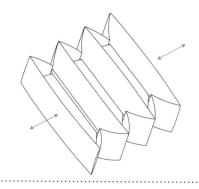

18. Practice collapsing and expanding to make the folds supple.

The Crown Book pushes the limits of the blizzard proportions to an extreme. By elongating the distance between the unit squares, what emerges are not pages, but rather a tall thin spine. New pages are inserted, nestling in the folds beneath the triangles.

COMPONENT	DIMENSIONS	QTY	PAPER
ACCORDION (SPINE/COVER)	7½ x 32 in. 19 x 80 cm	1	Text-weight paper: Elephant hide paper, 110 gsm
ACCORDION	5½ x 60 in. 14 x 152 cm	1	Text-weight paper on a roll
SINGLE FOLIOS (PAGES)	5½ x 7½ in. 14 x 19 cm	8	Text-weight paper: French Parchtone 60T

FINISHED DIMENSIONS:
5½ x 4 in. (14 x 10 cm)

TOOLS:
Self-healing cutting mat / Straight edge / Ruler / Sharp knife / Bone folder

TECHNIQUES:
Folding an Accordion 2–4–8, pages 30–32

Inside Reverse Fold, page 22

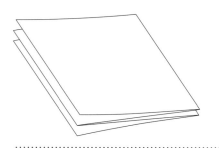

1. Fold the spine/cover sheet into a four-section accordion.

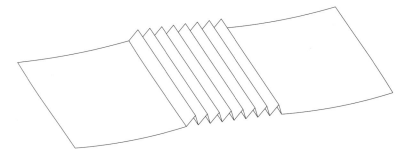

2. Fold the two middle sections into a 16-section accordion.

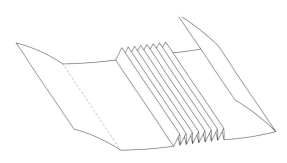

3. Fold the two outer sections in half. They will become the covers.

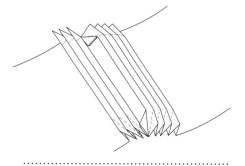

4. Fold right-angle triangles at the head and tail of the eight double sections, crease well and unfold again.

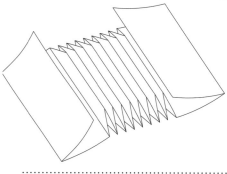

5. Inside reverse fold all the triangles.

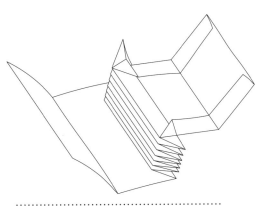

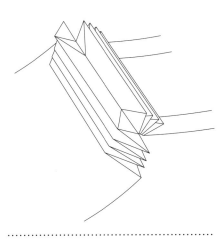

6. Gather up the sections, with one cover portion open to the right. Lift the top layer of triangles at the head and tail over to align their tips with the center fold, bringing the edges of the cover portion inward as shown. Fold the length of the cover and crease well.

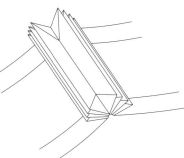

7. Open the remaining double sections one at a time, bringing the triangle tips inward to the center fold. Complete the left cover portion as in step 6.

8. You've created the spine and the covers.

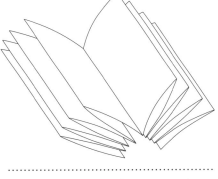

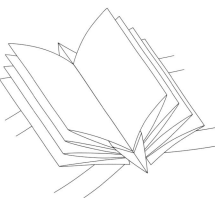

9. Retrieve the accordion pages strip and fold a 16-section accordion.

10. With the spine/cover assembly lying flat, open to the center sections and pull the triangles outward. Nestle the middle valley fold of the accordion pages within the open valley fold of the spine.

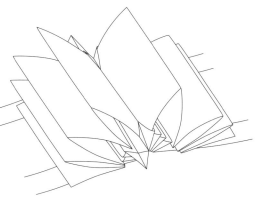

11. Bring the triangles down, locking the accordion pages in place, and move on to your left. Open the section, pull out the triangles and insert the next section of pages.

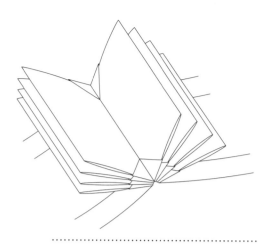

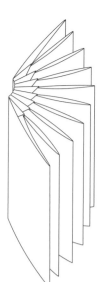

12. Repeat this process until all the accordion pages are evenly distributed and locked in place.

13. Insert the covers in the triangular pockets at the first and last accordion pages.

An alternative to using an accordion for pages is to use individual folios. If you are using folios, fold each one in half before proceeding. Below are two options for attaching.

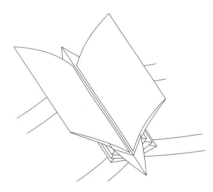

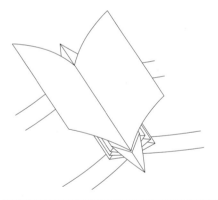

OPTION A: This option functions like the accordion pages with folds at the fore-edge. Instead of opening and closing on the valley fold, however, the pages are separate units and may shift without a little help offered by double-sided tape or adhesive. This is a good alternative to the accordion if a long strip of paper is unavailable or if, for example, you are printing text or images, as it may be easier to print folio pages than a long accordion.

OPTION B: Nestle the folios within each section of the Crown Book, with the fold at the spine. As with the accordion, the triangle locks the pages in place. You will notice that there are no folds at the fore-edge. The benefit of this option is that it yields double the amount of usable page area, as it uses both sides of the paper. We recommend using a soft, flexible and even a translucent paper for this option.

Here we demonstrate how a detail of one structure can be enlarged upon to take on a new function. The detail comes from the Crown Book, and instead of a 16-section accordion we use only four. We follow the same method of folding, just with fewer repeats. Though we've never done it, sometimes we imagine this structure at human scale.

COMPONENT	DIMENSIONS	QTY	PAPER
ACCORDION (SPINE/COVER)	<u>8</u> x 16 in. <u>20</u> x 40 cm	1	Text-weight paper: Elephant hide paper, 110 gsm
FOLIO (CARD)	<u>6</u> x 6 in. <u>15</u> x 15 cm	1	Light-weight paper: Tracing paper

FINISHED DIMENSIONS:
8 x 3 in. (20 x 7.5 cm)

TOOLS:
Self-healing cutting mat / Straight edge / Ruler / Sharp knife / Bone folder

TECHNIQUES:
Folding an Accordion, pages 30–32

Inverse Reverse Fold, page 22

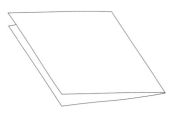

1. Fold the large sheet in half.

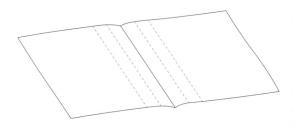

2. Measure one section of 2 in. (5 cm) on either side of the fold. Fold these sections in half to give a total of four sections.

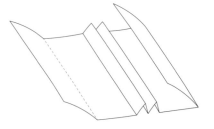

3. Fold these four sections into an accordion. Fold the two outer sections in half. These will become the covers.

4. Fold right-angle triangles at the head and tail of the two double sections, crease well and unfold again.

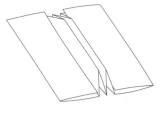

5. Inside reverse fold the four triangles.

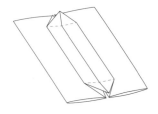

6. With the spine/cover assembly lying flat, open the double sections to the center with a cover on either side. Lift the triangles at the head and tail inward and align their tips with the center fold. Crease well.

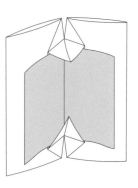

7. Fold the card in half. Lifting the triangles at the head and tail, nestle the fold of the card in the spine fold and bring the triangles down, locking it in place.

With the Blizzard Pocket we abandon the square, our faithful guide, and we turn to the rectangle as a layout tool. By making our initial folds at a slight angle instead of lining up with the fold, an interesting discovery was made. Gussets occur at the spine, allowing room for expansion, turning them into pockets. If you examine the Blizzard Pocket closely, you will find that it is actually a Blizzard Book turned around. We provide layout diagrams for this pocket version on page 69, or follow our example below.

COMPONENT	DIMENSIONS	QTY	PAPER
ACCORDION	<u>11</u> x 52 in. <u>28</u> x 128 cm	1	Paper on a roll: Butcher paper

FINISHED DIMENSIONS:
5½ x 3¼ in. (14 x 8 cm)

TOOLS:
Self-healing cutting mat / Straight edge / Ruler / Sharp knife / Bone folder / Pencil / Awl

TECHNIQUES:
Folding an Accordion 2–4–8, pages 30–32

Inside Reverse Fold, page 22

Marking with an Awl, page 18

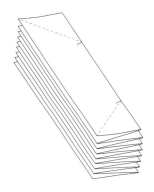

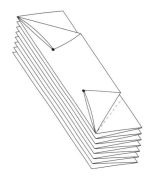

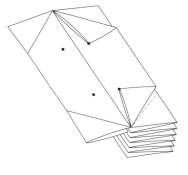

1. Fold a 16-section accordion. Mark 2¾ in. (7 cm) from the head and tail on the right edge of the top section of the accordion. Score from these marks to the corners and fold along the score lines on the top double section layer only.

2. Pierce with an awl at the point where the tips meet the center panel, piercing through the entire stack. These are shown as large dots for clarity, but they are in actuality very small pinpricks. Unfold the triangles.

3. Bring the double section to the left and fold the corners of the next double section to the awl marks. Unfold the triangles and bring the section to the left.

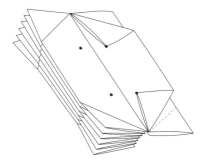

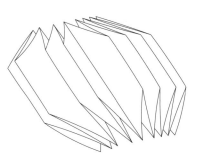

4. Continue until the corners of all double sections have been folded down to create triangles and then unfolded back again.

5. Inside reverse fold all the triangles.

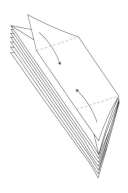

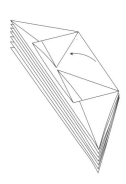

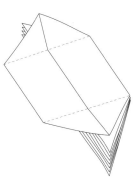

6. Turn the stack over and fold the head and tail triangle tips to meet at the center fold, creating a right-angle triangle.

7. The tips of the triangles should align with the edge of the stack and meet.

8. Turn the section to your left and repeat steps 6 and 7 with the double section, taking care to line up the triangle tips with the center fold.

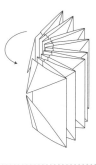

9. Continue until all triangles are folded in.

10. Stand the structure up. It resembles the Blizzard Book – but note that the pages are not connected at the spine. Rotating it toward you, spread the pages apart like a fan, causing the gussets to expand.

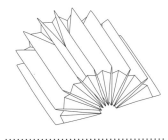

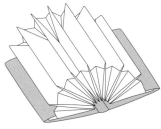

11. Set the structure down as shown, revealing the pockets. The pages are now gathered at the opposite side.

12. Insert cover into the outermost pockets. See note for cover options.

A flexible cover option is the School-Book Wrapper, pages 172–75. Or construct a cover from a piece of cardstock cut to the height of the book and four times the width. Center the spine, make folds at the fore-edges and insert the ends into the outermost pockets.

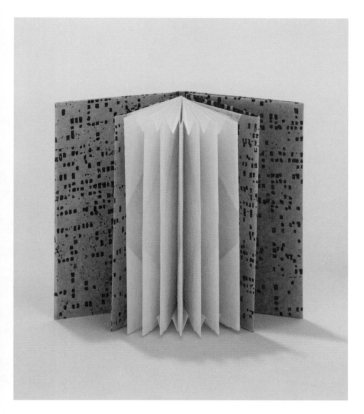

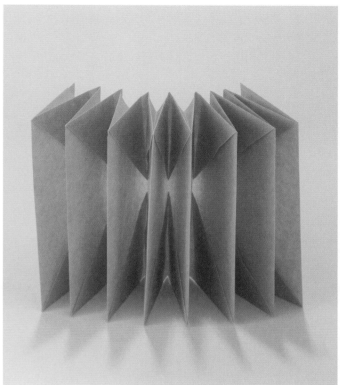

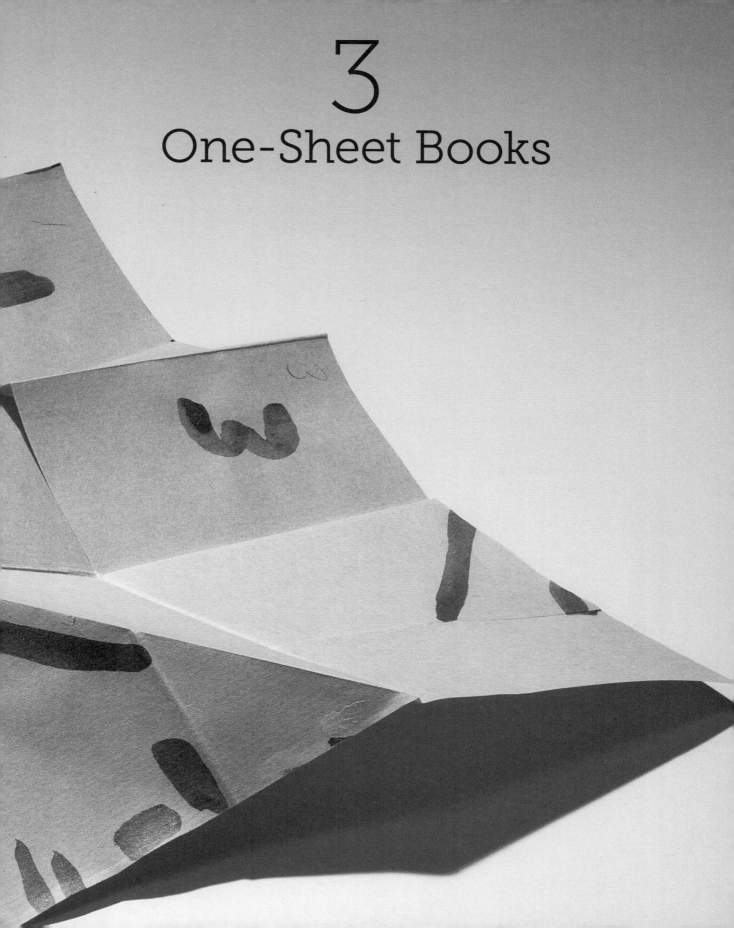

3
One-Sheet Books

One-Sheet Books

Many of the techniques and projects in this chapter arise from an interest in and fascination with origami, map folds and other applications of collapsible folds. A book folded from a single sheet of paper, including covers, offers a unique opportunity to consider the content and cover as one comprehensive design exercise. We explore the coming together of printing, layout and folding. One-sheet books are a means to transform a large print (composition) into smaller divisions for a book-like sequential viewing. It is helpful to make a mock-up first, number the

pages and identify the covers to guide you with the placement of areas to be printed. Depending on the book structure you choose, some of the pages will be upside down in the layout and a few end up on the back of the paper. The cover design may be broken up and appear in several places. Once the book is folded, however, everything falls into place. Consider these structures for group collaborations in which each person designs a page. To generate more spontaneous content, drawing, painting and writing are alternatives to printing.

The conventions of our drawings are not meant to be exactly the same as those found in origami books, but you will notice strategic arrows to help you through the steps – some of which are tricky to fold. For this chapter, it would be helpful to familiarize yourself with the concept of the inside reverse fold, the squash fold, mountain and valley folds, and dividing into even and odd numbers of parts in our techniques section (pages 18–25).

Four projects in this chapter have a proportional relationship between the height and width of the initial paper size built in to their success. To scale the size of structure up or down, we use a unit square for layout. Increase or decrease the size of the unit square and then multiply by the number of squares shown in the following diagrams.

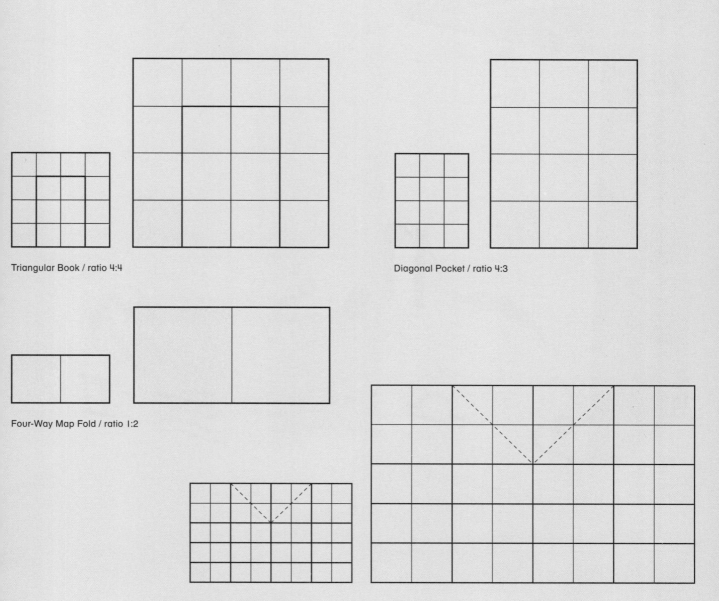

Triangular Book / ratio 4:4

Diagonal Pocket / ratio 4:3

Four-Way Map Fold / ratio 1:2

Franklin Fold / ratio 5:8

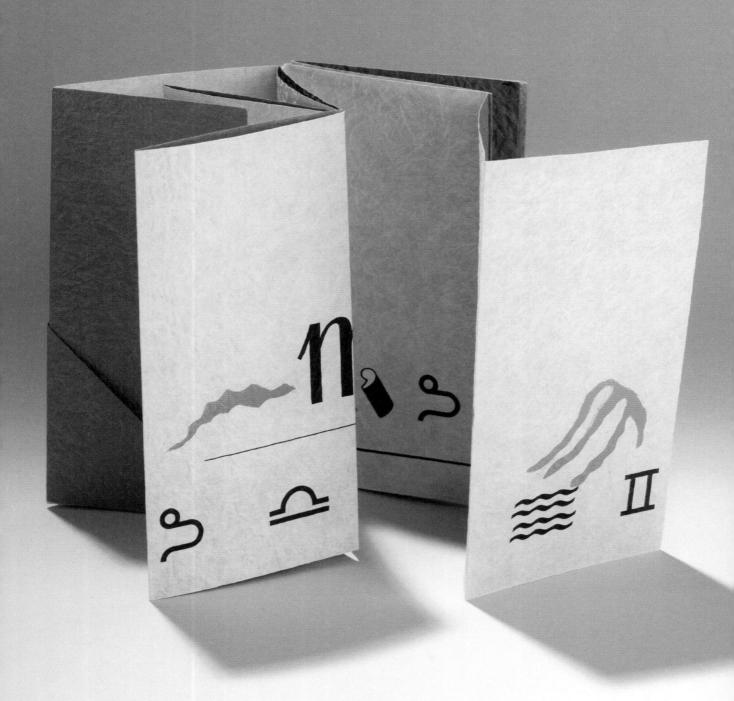

The Franklin Fold was developed as a keepsake inspired by a series of drawings from Benjamin Franklin's "On the Art of Swimming". What is special about this structure is that the covers, six pages and two center accordion fold-outs are all made from a single sheet of paper – an ideal format for the layout of a poem or a short story. We've engineered the proportions of the initial sheet of paper to be roughly equal to those of the golden rectangle.

NOTE:
To scale the size of this structure up or down, refer to the diagram provided in the introduction to this chapter.

FINISHED DIMENSIONS:
5½ x 3 in. (14 x 7.5 cm)

TOOLS:
Self-healing cutting mat
Straight edge / Ruler / Sharp knife
Bone folder / 4 paper clips
Double-sided tape / Pencil

TECHNIQUE:
Folding an Accordion 2–4–8, pages 30–32

COMPONENT	DIMENSIONS	QTY	PAPER
ACCORDION	13¾ x 22 in. 35 x 56 cm	1	Text-weight paper: Japanese Momi paper, 90G

1. Fold the paper into a four-section accordion.

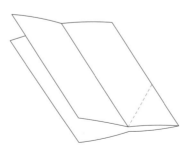

2. Bring the upper and lower sections to the left. The right side of the paper is facing out.

3. Fold the corner at the middle double section diagonally to the left, lining it up with the vertical fold and creating a large triangle.

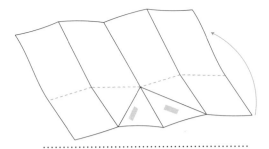

4. Open up so that the wrong side of paper is facing up. (Optional: Apply a piece of double-sided tape to each side of the large triangle. Leave the paper backing on the tape.)

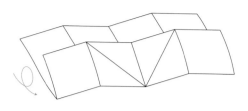

5. Lining up the folds and edges, fold the portion with the triangle up. Flip the sheet over.

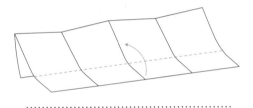

6. Using the vertical folds and side edges as guides, bring the bottom edge up until it is flush with the edge below.

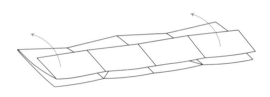

7. Crease well, creating a mountain fold along this edge.

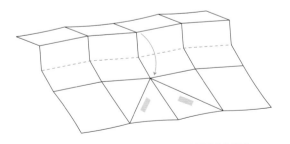

8. Lift this mountain fold to bring the portion up. Bring it back down to align with the fold at the tip of the triangle. Press down and crease well.

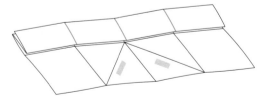

9. Make cuts through all three layers, as shown in the diagram. These four stacks will become the pages of your book.

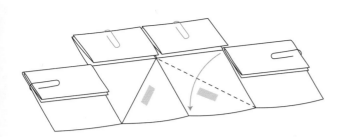

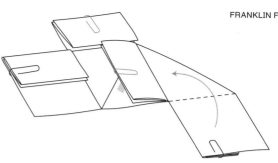

10. Flip the two outer stacks toward you. Secure all four stacks with paper clips. It might be helpful to use two colors of paper clips. Note the orientation of the paper clips.

11. Fold the right-hand side of the large triangle down along the existing diagonal fold. Bring the paper-clipped square up.

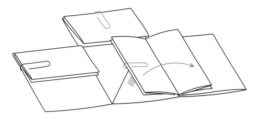

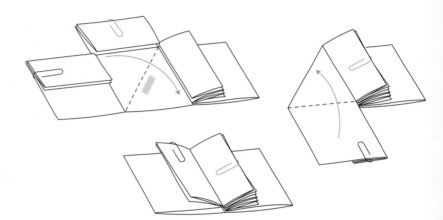

12. One section of pages is in place. Remove the paper clip. Bring the adjacent section of pages over to the right and remove the paper clip.

13. Repeat steps 11 through 13 on the left side, reversing direction.

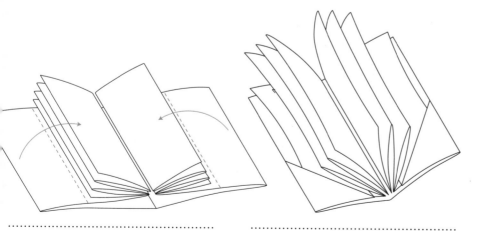

14. With the pages lying flat, mark the covers ¼ in. (5 mm) from the fore-edge of the pages. Gently fold the covers at this mark.

15. Lifting the pages up, insert the first and last pages into the triangular pockets inside the covers.

If the pages are uneven, straighten them out at the bottom. The unevenness will be moved to the top, where they can be trimmed as necessary. We add double-sided tape at a place where the book tends to open up. Once taped, however, it can no longer be taken apart for demonstration purposes. Therefore, consider this an option and only remove the paper backing from the tape when the book is finished and trimmed if necessary.

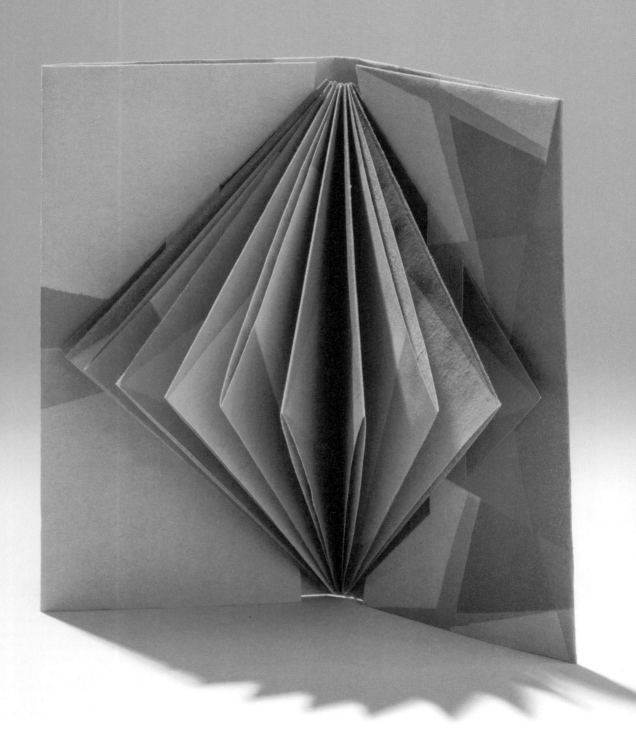

Triangles are ubiquitous in one-sheet book folding and therefore it is not surprising that we introduce our version of a Triangular Book. Dividing squares by folding them along the diagonal transforms the static nature of a row of squares into a more dynamic, slinky-like form. This model was originally conceived of for a silkscreen workshop with ten participants, each having one square to design. The middle part had the proper proportions to become the cover, resulting in the entire sheet being used with no waste. Such collaborations are fun and stimulating and a lot of ground gets covered between layout, printing and folding. The proportion of the initial sheet of paper is a square and can be of any size; just keep in mind that this structure starts out with a large square and becomes small very quickly.

COMPONENT	DIMENSIONS	QTY	PAPER
SQUARE	<u>15</u> x 15 in. <u>38</u> x 38 cm	I	Text-weight paper: Kraft paper

FINISHED DIMENSIONS:
5½ x 2¾ in. (14 x 7 cm)

TOOLS:
Self-healing cutting mat / Straight edge / Sharp knife / 16-in. (40-cm) ruler / Bone folder / Pencil / Paper clips

TECHNIQUE:
Making Non-Tear Slits with Anchor Holes, page 21

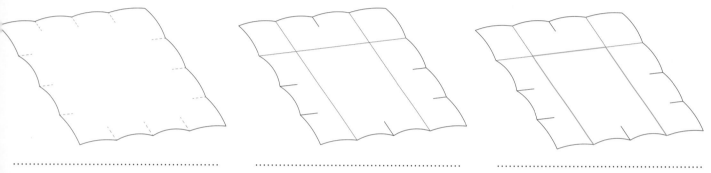

1. With the right side of the paper facing down, divide the square into 16 small squares. Make your creases all valleys and no longer than 2 in. (5 cm). Do not crease all the way across or down.

2. Mark as shown with three light pencil lines.

3. Cut out the inner rectangle and set aside – this will become the cover.

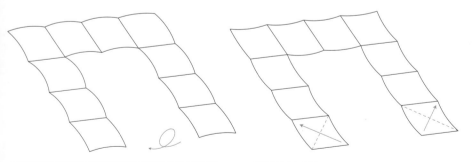

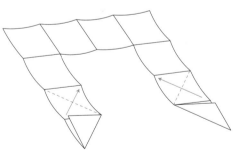

4. Complete the creases started in step 1 so that they are all nicely articulated valley folds.

5. Turn the piece over, showing only mountain folds. Starting at the bottom, work with both "legs" simultaneously, as they work in mirror image. Fold the first two squares diagonally in half, away from each other. Take care to get the direction of this fold correct.

6. Bring both triangles in toward each other, creating the next diagonal valley fold. Crease.

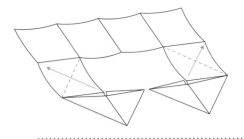

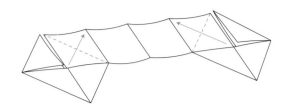

7. Fold the triangles up and away from each other. Crease.

8. Fold the triangles up and toward each other to create two squares. Crease.

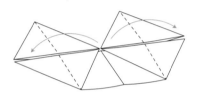

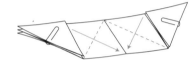

9. Fold the squares in half, away from each other, creating two triangles again.

10. Divide these triangles in half again by bringing the upper parts down toward you.

11. At this stage, it is helpful to use paper clips to secure the stacks of triangles. Bring the outer tips of the triangles toward each other and at an angle toward you. Crease.

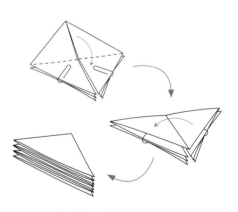

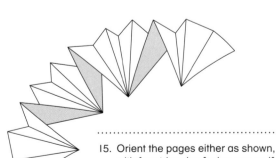

12. Bring the rear triangle forward along the existing fold lines.

13. Fold in half one last time. The text block is now complete. The long leg of the triangle is effectively the spine.

14. Remove the paper clips.

15. Orient the pages either as shown, with four triangles facing you or, if you have something printed, you can rotate it. There is no top and bottom to this structure. Reassemble as a compact triangle and place under weight while preparing your covers.

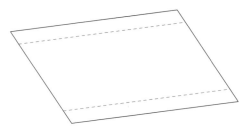

16. Retrieve the saved cover piece. Fold in 1 in. (2.5 cm) at the head and tail of the long dimension.

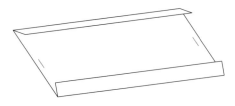

17. Measure the thickness of your spine and transfer this measurement to the short dimensions of the cover piece.

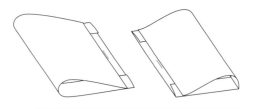

18. Fold the left side over to the right mark and crease. Fold the right side over to the left mark and crease. A spine thickness is created at the center.

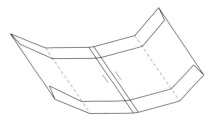

19. Make two marks, approximately ¼ in. (5 mm) on either side of the spine folds and bring the corresponding edges to that mark. Crease well.

20. To create slits to hold the book in place, nestle the book block (the triangles) inside the cover. Position a ⅜-in. (1-cm) strip of paper between the text block and the cover. With a sharp pencil, mark each side of the strip where it meets the triangles, approximately in the middle of the cover. Repeat this step on the other cover.

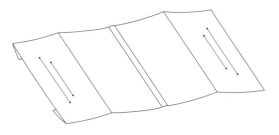

21. Remove the text block, open up the cover and cut slits between the marks made in the previous step.

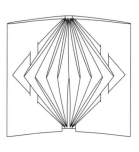

22. Refold the cover along its original crease lines and place the text block inside the cover again, inserting the first and last pages through the corresponding slits.

The Four-Way Map Fold originated as a model for a workshop focusing on map folds. Allowing sections to fold out while other sections remain folded results in an infinite number of possibilities in viewing of the overall "map". This project benefits from making a model first to figure out directionality and the placement of images. The proportion of the initial sheet of paper is always two squares.

COMPONENT	DIMENSIONS	QTY	PAPER
RECTANGLE	5½ x 11 in. 14 x 28 cm	1	Text-weight paper: Kraft paper
COVER	5½ x 3 in. 14 x 7.5 cm	2	Cover-weight paper or cardstock: Japanese linen cardstock, 244g

NOTE

To scale the size of this structure up or down, refer to the diagram provided in the introduction to this chapter.

FINISHED DIMENSIONS:
5½ x 3 in. (14 x 7.5 cm)

TOOLS:

Self-healing cutting mat / Straight edge / Ruler / Sharp knife / Bone folder / Pencil / Colored markers or pencils / Double-sided tape

TECHNIQUES:

Folding an Accordion 2–4–8, pages 30–32

Inside Reverse Fold, page 22

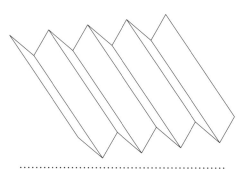

1. Fold an eight-section accordion. Open the accordion with three mountain folds and four valley folds. The right side of the sheet should be facing up.

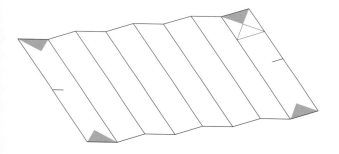

2. Color in four triangles at the locations shown in the diagram. These will help orient you in the folding steps to follow. Mark the center of the short sides.

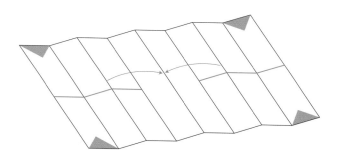

3. Line a straight edge between the two center marks and make cuts as shown, being careful not to cut the two center sections. Bring the right and left mountain folds to meet at the center mountain fold.

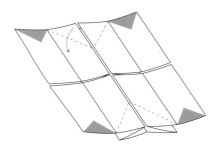

4. Fold the four corners at the center diagonally, lining them up with a fold for accuracy. Crease well.

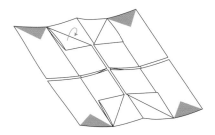

5. Open up and inside reverse fold the four triangles you've just made.

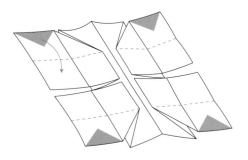

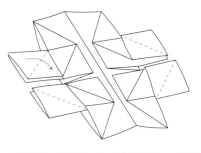

6. Fold the four top layers of the upper and lower sections to the cut edges.

7. Fold the four outer small squares into triangles, as shown. Crease well.

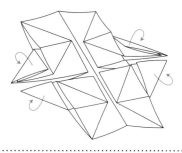

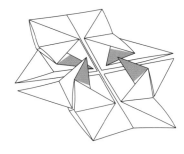

8. At each of these four locations, open up and inside reverse fold the triangles you've just made.

9. Lift the upper triangle and inside reverse fold again toward the center until the colored-in triangle reappears.

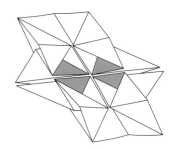

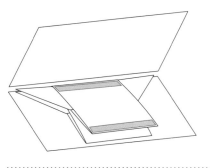

10. There are four triangles remaining, as shown in our model. We attached covers at this point; alternatively, you can inside reverse fold those triangles into the body of the square format.

11. Optional covers are added by folding the map in half and attaching to the two covers with double-sided tape.

Originally inspired by the seven-section dos-à-dos booklet fold (page 123), one can see the evolution of the Fishbone structure. By pushing the limits, extending the cut and non-cut areas and adding more panels, an arrangement resembling a fishbone developed. This structure utilizes a variation of the box pleat. It also shares characteristics with a map fold known as the Falk Fold, patented in 1951 by G.E.A. Falk.

This structure can be used in a flat book format, with the "pages" able to turn in a traditional way. We often stand it up, however, pulling the leading section as a tab. The result is a cascading display of the pages. By gently pushing back on this tab, the pages snap into their original position. The Fishbone's ability to extend out makes it uniquely suited to displaying content on both sides simultaneously.

COMPONENT	DIMENSIONS	QTY	PAPER
RECTANGLE	13 x 21 in. 33 x 51 cm	1	Text-weight paper in the range of 40 to 110 gsm: Fabriano Ingres 90 gsm

FINISHED DIMENSIONS:
6½ x 4⅛ in. (16.5 x 10.5 cm)

TOOLS:
Self-healing cutting mat / Straight edge / Ruler / Sharp knife / Bone folder / Pencil / Double-sided tape

TECHNIQUE:
Knife Pleats and Box Pleats, page 23

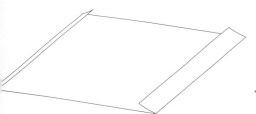

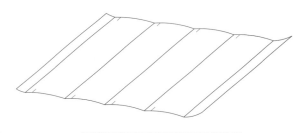

1. The right side of the paper should be facing up. Fold up 1 in. (2.5 cm) on the left side and 2 in. (5 cm) on the right, creating extensions, right and left.

2. Fold the remaining portion into four sections by folding the sheet in half and then in half again. These are all valley folds.

3. Open up. Starting from the right and skipping the first fold, mark ½ in. (1.5 cm) to the right of each fold, as shown.

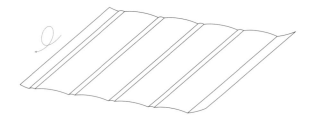

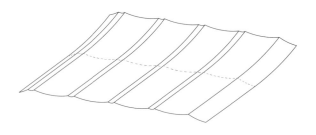

4. Using a straight edge, score and crease from mark to mark, creating four new valley folds defining four narrow sections. All folds are valley folds.

5. Flip the sheet over toward you so that the valley folds are now mountain folds and the 2-in. (5-cm) extension is still on your right. Fold the sheet in half lengthwise and open up.

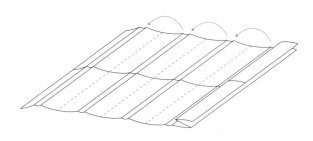

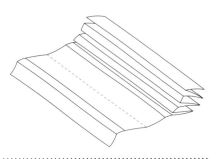

6. From the right-hand side, begin pleating by bringing the first mountain fold to the second one.

7. Skipping the ½-in. (1.5-cm) section, bring the next mountain fold to the next. You are halving the larger sections each time. Continue to pleat until the end of the sequence.

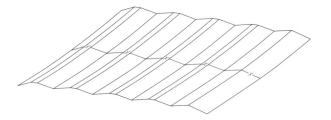

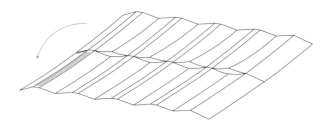

8. Open the paper up and mark the right extension and the four ½-in. (1.5-cm) sections with an X, as shown. Following the diagram, cut along the horizontal fold between the X-marked sections, being careful not to cut into the X-marked sections themselves.

9. Apply a strip of double-sided tape to half of the last narrow section, as shown. Bring the top half of the sheet toward you and remove the backing paper from the double-sided tape to adhere the top half to the bottom half.

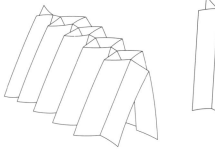

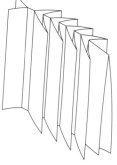

10. Stand the piece up. Gently pushing in from the right extension, collapse the pages into the fishbone form.

Though this structure stands quite well on its own, we often give it a cover. We suggest the Diagonal Pocket (pages 116–19), using the extension fold as a location to sew the book into the cover. Another option is the School-Book Wrapper (pages 172–75). Attach card covers for stiffness to the extensions using double-sided tape. Once the cards are in place, make a wrapper to fit these dimensions and slide the card covers into the pockets.

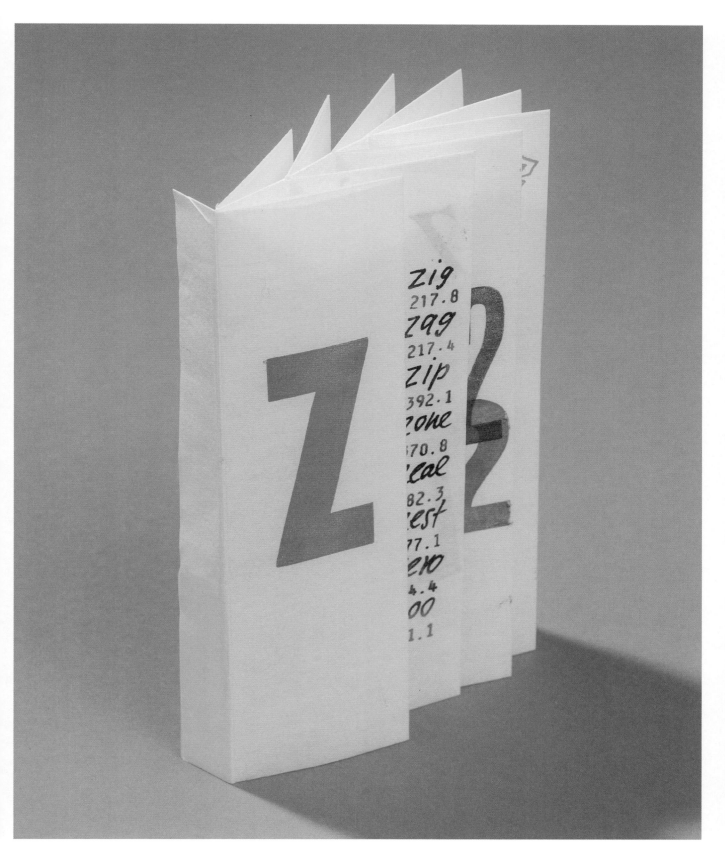

The Tree Fold is a further development of the Fishbone Fold, increasing the width of the pages while keeping the uncut sections uniform. Just like the Fishbone, it utilizes a variation of the box pleat fold. If you are mathematically inclined, try a variation by increasing the widths of both the cut and the uncut sections.

COMPONENT	DIMENSIONS	QTY	PAPER
RECTANGLE	<u>13</u> x 25 in. <u>33</u> x 62 cm	1	Lightweight paper: Japanese Obonai Feather, 45 g

FINISHED DIMENSIONS:
6½ x 3⅝ in. (16.5 x 8.5 cm)

TOOLS:
Self-healing cutting mat /
Straight edge / Ruler / Sharp knife /
Bone folder / Awl / Pencil /
Double-sided tape

TECHNIQUES:
Knife Pleats and Box Pleats, page 23

Inside Reverse Fold, page 22

Sewing (optional), page 24

FOLDING SEQUENCE
½ in. / 2 in. / ½ in. / 3 in. / ½ in. / 4 in. / ½ in. / 5 in. / ½ in. /
6 in. / ½ in. / extension

1.5 cm / 5 cm / 1.5 cm / 7.5 cm / 1.5 cm / 10 cm / 1.5 cm /
12.5 cm / 1.5 cm / 15 cm / 1.5 cm / extension

The ½-in. (1.5-cm) sections stay the same, while the spaces between them progressively increase. There will be an extra section left over, which we'll call the left extension.
This extension will be used later as a hinge.

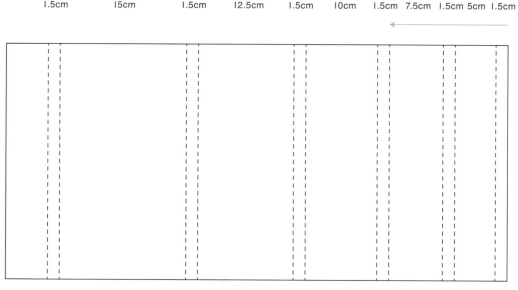

1. The right side of the paper should be facing you. Starting from the right side of the sheet, mark the distances according to the folding sequence above, smallest dimensions first, increasing as you go. Score, crease and make all the folds valley folds.

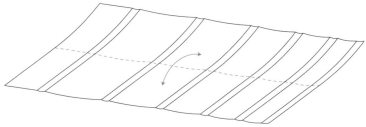

2. Flip the sheet over so that the valley folds are now mountain folds. Fold the sheet in half lengthwise and open it up.

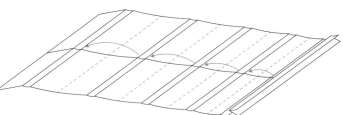

3. From the right-hand edge, begin pleating by bringing the first mountain fold to the second one.

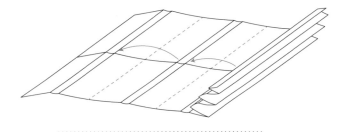

4. Skipping the ½-in. (1.5-cm) section, bring the next mountain fold to the next. You are halving the larger sections each time.

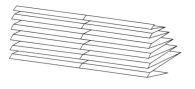

5. Continue to pleat in this manner until the end of the sequence.

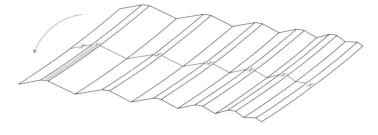

6. Open the paper up. Mark the left and right extensions and each ½-in. (1.5-cm) section with an X. Following the diagram, cut along the horizontal fold between the X-marked sections, being careful not to cut into the X-marked sections themselves. Apply a strip of double-sided tape on half of the last narrow section, as shown.

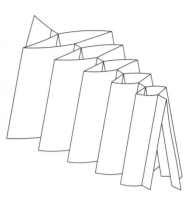

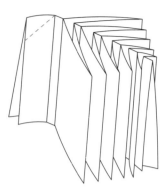

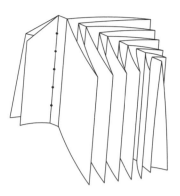

7. Bring the top half of the rectangle toward you and remove the backing paper from the double-sided tape to adhere the top half to the bottom half. Stand the piece up.

8. Gently pushing in from the right extension, collapse the pages into the tree form. Make a diagonal fold on the left extension. Inside reverse fold the resulting triangle. This will give you two separate hinges to which individual covers may be attached.

9. The extension may also be folded over to one side and used as a hinge. Pierce holes in the fold and sew the Tree Fold into a cover such as the Diagonal Pocket (pages 116–19). See Sewing in Techniques (page 24).

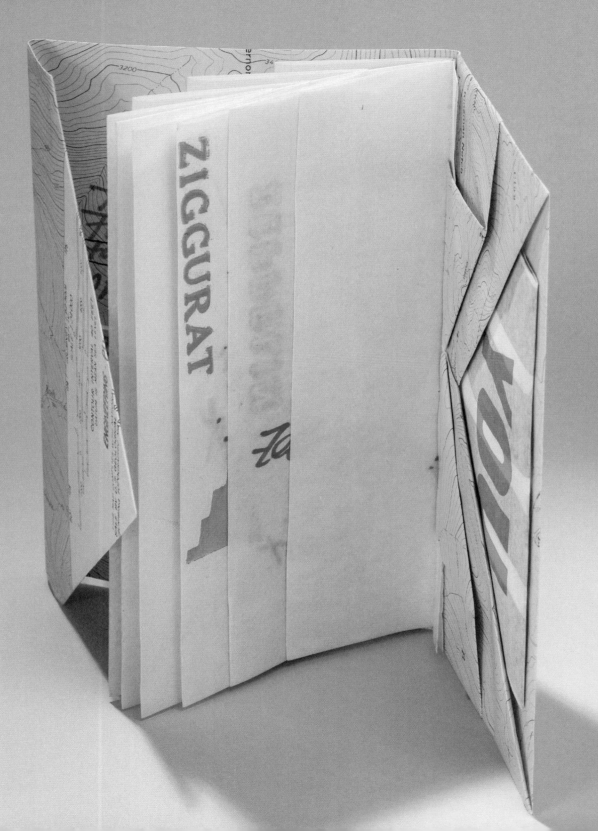

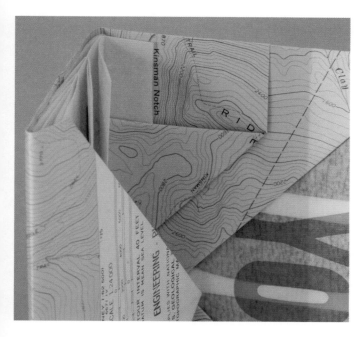

COMPONENT	DIMENSIONS	QTY	PAPER
RECTANGLE	<u>9</u> x 12 in. <u>24</u> x 32 cm	I	Text-weight paper: Topographic map

FINISHED DIMENSIONS:
4½ x 3 in. (12 x 8 cm)

TOOLS:
Self-healing cutting mat / Straight edge / Ruler / Sharp knife / Bone folder / Pencil

TECHNIQUE:
Squash Fold, page 23

With its multiple pockets, the Diagonal Pocket is an ideal structure to have on hand to keep documents or collect ephemera. It employs classic origami techniques such as the squash fold, as well as the tucking method used in finishing the flap that slides into the front pocket. Used as a cover, it can have something as simple as a few pages or a slightly more complex Tree Fold (see pages 112–15) sewn into its spine.

To increase or decrease the size of this structure, use a sheet where the ratio of height to width is 3:4. To use this structure as a cover for a book, measure the height and width of the book. Cut the sheet for the cover following this equation: 2 x height by 4 x width. If you are not measuring for a specific content, use a sheet whose ratio is 3:4.

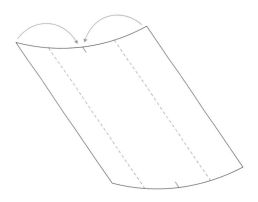

1. Mark the shorter sides of the paper at the midpoint with a small pencil line or a pinch.

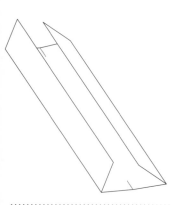

2. Fold the long edges to the midpoint marks. Open up.

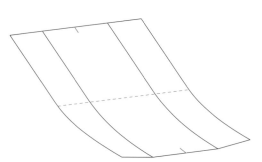

3. Fold the sheet in half across the shorter dimension, creating a valley fold.

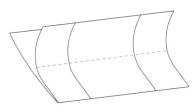

4. Bring the top layer back to the folded edge, creating a mountain fold.

5. Lift the mountain fold up
   and toward you.

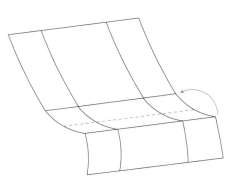

6. Bring the mountain fold
   to the valley fold directly
   above it, creating a pleat
   underneath.

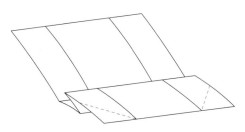

7. Fold the two bottom corners
   diagonally, lining them up
   with the existing vertical
   folds, and crease well.

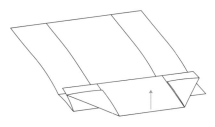

8. Temporarily fold this section
   up, revealing the pleat
   underneath.

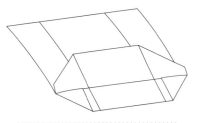

9. Fold the two corners of
   the pleat diagonally, lining
   them up with the horizontal
   fold above.

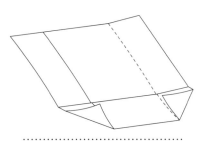

10. Bring the section above
    back down, as shown.

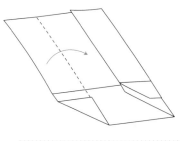

11. Using the two vertical valley
    folds created earlier, bring
    the right and left sides
    toward the center.

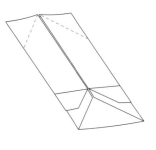

12. Fold the two top corners
    down so that they meet
    at the center.

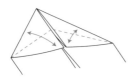

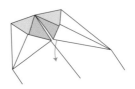

13. This creates two triangles at the top of your sheet. Divide these triangles by folding the bottom edges up to align with the diagonal sides. Unfold again.

14. You'll observe an opening on each side of the two triangles where they meet.

15. Open these up and move the top layers away from each other toward the diagonal edges to create squash folds, flattening as you go.

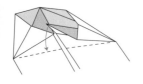

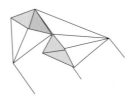

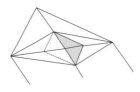

16. Lift the right squash fold on the lower edge and gently pull it all the way down until it is flattened out again and is perpendicular to the main body of the structure.

17. Repeat with the left squash fold.

18. The two squash folds align with each other. Fit the tip of one fold into the other.

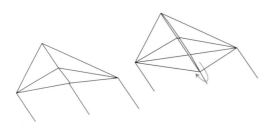

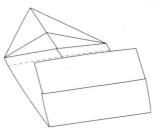

19. Holding the two squash folds together at the center line, tuck them underneath. This creates a nice solution to prevent unfolding.

20. Fold the lower portion of the pocket along the pre-creased fold and bring the triangle at the top over to create an enclosure. Make this last one a soft fold, not sharply creased. Tuck the point of the triangle into the pleat.

This project begins with an eight-page booklet ingeniously created from a single sheet of paper, four folds and one cut. Its origin is unknown, but it is frequently encountered – and so, too, are various adaptations. By increasing the number of sections and playing with the positioning of the cuts, spatial qualities emerge that we are particularly intrigued by and hope will encourage you to experiment as well. The intrinsic simplicity of this family of structures makes them highly versatile in their applications – one sheet of paper and a knife or scissors are all that are really needed. It is an ideal project to introduce to children as a first step toward bookmaking and publishing. They can lay out the book on one sheet and it can be easily reproduced. These structures can be made from any sized sheet of paper, though a rectangle that is not a square produces slightly better proportions.

We begin with and notate the original and simplest form – the four-section booklet – followed by diagrams of variations we've developed. The four-section booklet begins with a four-section accordion, while the other three begin with eight-section accordions.

NOTE:
Pre-cut paper sizes such as 8½ x 11 in. or 11 x 17 in. (A4 or A3) are ideal to start with.

COMPONENT	DIMENSIONS	QTY	PAPER
ACCORDION	<u>11</u> x <u>17</u> in. <u>29.7</u> x <u>42</u> cm/A3 or any size rectangle	1	Text-weight paper: French Speckletone, Dur-O-Tone and Parchtone 70T, 60T

FINISHED DIMENSIONS:
Variable

TOOLS:
Self-healing cutting mat / Straight edge / Sharp knife / Ruler / Bone folder / Pencil / Brush and paint or colored pens (optional)

TECHNIQUES:
Folding an Accordion 2–4–8, pages 30–32

Folding an Accordion 3–6–12, pages 33–34

1. Fold a four-section accordion.

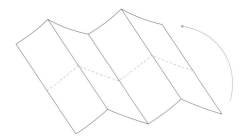

2. Position it so that the two mountain folds are facing up. Fold the sheet horizontally in half away from you.

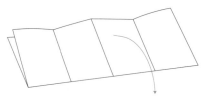

3. Open the accordion up toward you.

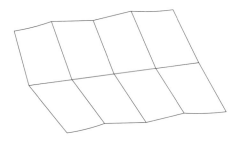

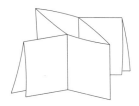

4. Cut along the horizontal valley fold, leaving the first and last sections intact.

5. Lift, bringing the top half toward you, standing it up. Gently push both ends toward the center until a "room" emerges.

6. Push a little further and an eight-page booklet emerges. Crease well around the spine to give it crispness.

Eight-Section Centre Cut

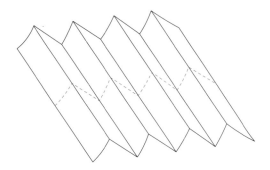

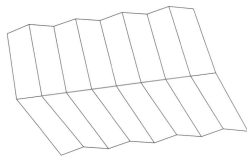

By increasing the number of sections of your accordion to eight and making the cuts in different locations, you will see how this structure yields a variety of outcomes. Follow the method outlined above and experiment!

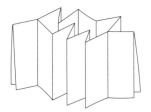

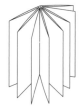

Eight-Section Offset Cut

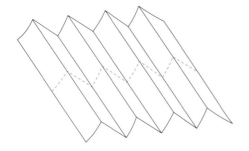

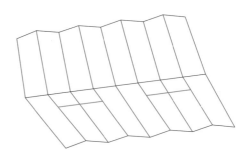

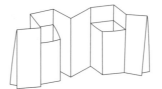

By offsetting the location where cuts are made, a three-dimensional spatial effect is achieved.

Seven-Section Dos-à-dos

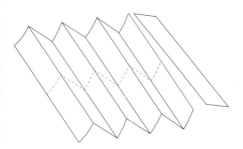

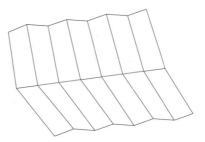

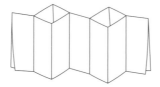

In this example we remove one section of the accordion, resulting in a dos-à-dos — a double booklet back to back.

This variation of the booklet fold family is one that we've designed to be particularly three-dimensional, adding pop-ups and a star form. A dramatic effect is created from the simple repetition of the same pop-up six times. The interior space at the center of this structure is as compelling as the pop-ups that fold outward. The use of color, collage and drawings can only intensify the resulting effect. Using paper with a translucent quality allows lights to filter into the center and adds another dimension. The pop-up we describe below is simplified for clarity's sake. We recommend experimenting with pop-up techniques, as even the simplest pop-ups are tricky to achieve without some trial and error first. Fold a scrap of paper in half, cut several pieces to the height and width of one section, and draw a vertical center line. It is important not to extend beyond the center line of the page or they will, when collapsed, extend beyond the confines of the page.

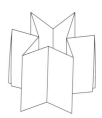

COMPONENT	DIMENSIONS	QTY	PAPER
ACCORDION	11 x 17 in. <u>29.7</u> x 42 cm/A3 or any size rectangle	1	Lightweight or text-weight paper: Handmade hardy paper

FINISHED DIMENSIONS:
Variable

TECHNIQUE:
Folding an Accordion 3–6–12, pages 33–34

TOOLS:
Self-healing cutting mat / Straight edge / Sharp knife / Ruler / Bone folder Pencil / Brush and paint or colored pens (optional)

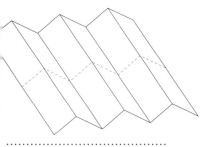

1. Fold a six-section accordion. With three mountain folds facing up, fold the sheet horizontally in half away from you.

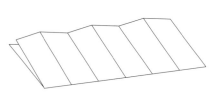

2. Open the accordion up toward you.

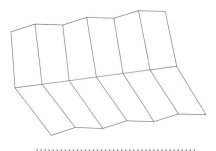

3. Cut along the horizontal valley fold, leaving the first and sixth sections intact.

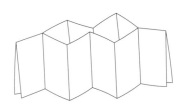

4. Lift, bringing the top half toward you, standing it up.

5. Gently push both ends toward the center until a star shape emerges. This is the basic shape of our form.

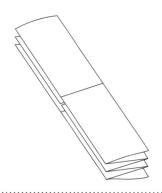

6. Unfold the star form and bring it back to the accordion in step 1.

7. Create a template for your pop-up. The template should be half the height of the accordion. It should also tell you what is a cut line and what is a fold line to avoid confusion.

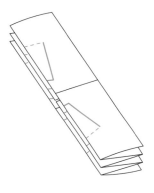

8. With the three mountain folds facing left, trace your pop-up template in mirror image onto the upper and lower halves of the top section of the accordion.

9. If your paper is thin, cut through all layers at once. If it is thick, trace the template on all three layers in the same orientation.

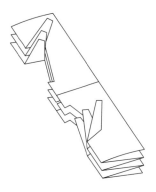

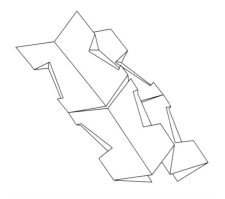

10. Fold the pop-ups in both directions, creasing well.

11. Push the pop-ups in.

12. As in steps 4 and 5, return the piece to the star form, pulling the pop-ups into position. They should be popping outward. Experiment with a variety of shapes. For additional surprise effects, add color to either the inside or outside faces of the pop-ups.

4
Albums

Albums

The photo album as we know it is quickly disappearing with the advent of the digital age. We have virtual repositories of images along with a selection of customizable templates for online viewing. However, as long as we remain in the tactile world, there is still a need for physical repositories to house objects and ephemera we encounter and want to preserve. We often refer to albums as storage books. In contrast to books that are permanently bound at the spine, albums are all about storing and displaying an array of materials in a way that allows the content to be removed, replaced or re-shuffled easily. Many albums also address the challenge of incorporating low-relief and, to some degree, three-dimensional objects.

These materials require adequate space for their display. This has been addressed over centuries, often resulting in highly complex, heavy-duty structures. Our response is to offer alternatives that are in line with our approach to lightweight and primarily non-adhesive formats. The examples in this chapter specifically address album structures that can display, for example, a finite grouping of images (the Panorama Book); that can accommodate objects that have some dimension or benefit from having air and space around them (the Spider Book); and that address the expandability issue as a collection of items can easily grow over time (the Piano Hinge).

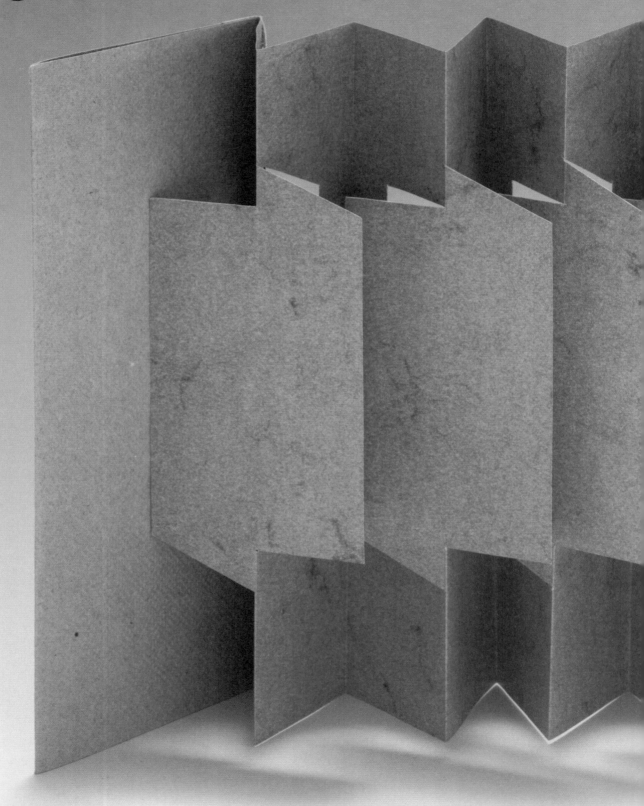

One can think of the Panorama Book as a portable gallery. When standing, the broad flat panels create a continuous array of the book's contents. Cut from a single sheet of paper, small portions of the accordion's mountain folds are utilized as hinges, allowing the panels to semi-rotate on their axis. The negative spaces of the panels become windows, allowing light and shadow to play upon all surfaces.

By making the model we describe, one comes to understand how the panels and hinges work together, and it is possible to cut panels within panels or oddly shaped panels. We provide some variations we've come up with and encourage you to experiment with the endless display possibilities of this structure.

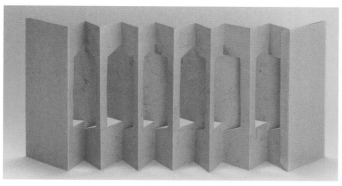

COMPONENT	DIMENSIONS	QTY	PAPER
ACCORDION	8 x 25½ in. / 20 x 64 cm	1	Text-weight paper: Elephant hide paper, 110 gsm
COVERS	8 x 8 in. / 20 x 20 cm	2	Cover-weight paper: Handmade Zaansch bord
TEMPLATE	8 x 4 in. / 20 x 10 cm	1	Cardstock: Japanese linen cardstock, 244g

FINISHED DIMENSIONS:
8 x 4 in. (20 x 10 cm)

TOOLS:
Self-healing cutting mat / Straight edge / Sharp knife / Paper cutter (optional) / Awl / Scissors / Bone folder / Pencil / Double-sided tape

TECHNIQUES:
Folding an Accordion with Extensions, pages 35–39

Marking with an Awl, page 18

Measuring Devices: Templates, page 19

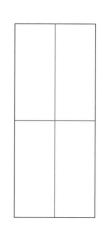

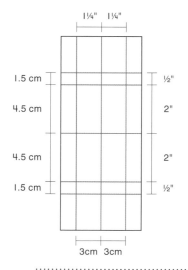

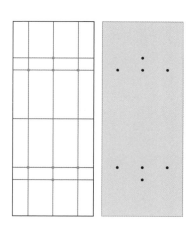

1. Prepare the template. Divide the panel in half horizontally and vertically, drawing center lines.

2. Working outward from these two lines, make additional lines as indicated in the diagram.

3. At the locations indicated by dots, pierce with an awl.

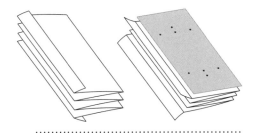

4. Fold a six-section accordion with ¾-in. (2-cm) extensions. Place the template on top of the accordion, with the hinges to your left. Using an awl, pierce small holes through the whole stack at the marked locations.

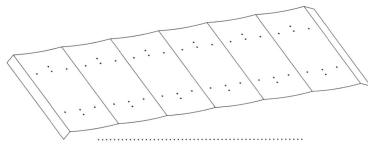

5. Remove the template and, pulling it to the right, spread the accordion out flat. The wrong side of the accordion is now facing up. Turn the three valley folds into mountain folds so that all the folds are now mountain folds.

6. Placing a straight edge along the center awl marks on each panel, make score lines as indicated, taking care not to score in the central panel area.

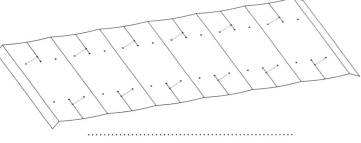

7. Make diagonal cuts by connecting holes and following the diagram.

8. Make horizontal cuts as shown.

9. Finally, make vertical cuts. The sections are now ready for folding.

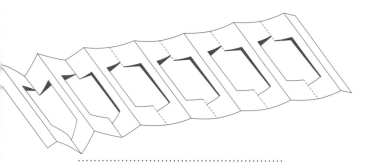

10. Starting at the left side, bring the first mountain fold to this edge. Take care not to fold the panel, allowing it to lie flat. Repeat with the remaining mountain folds. Sharpen all the folds with your bone folder.

11. Fold the covers in half, noting that the grain should run parallel to the fold, and attach them to the front and back hinges with double-sided tape.

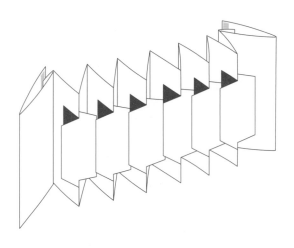

12. When complete, stand the book up and expand it to reveal an array of panels. Note that a small portion of the fold at the bottom of the panel needs to be creased to the left, allowing the panel to swing back and forth. Attach content to the panels.

VARIATION
Once you've practiced this structure and its hinging mechanism, experiment with asymmetrically shaped panels or panels within panels decreasing in size.

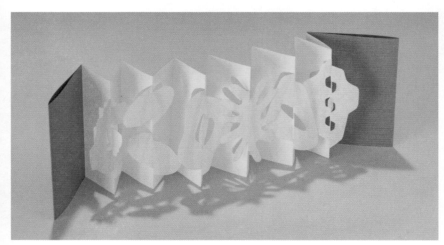

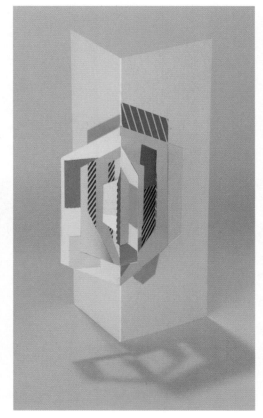

In a folding workshop many years ago, an architect, Per Tamsen, showed us a folding sequence he had developed that in turn inspired us to create this structure. By increasing the spaces between mountain and valley folds, space is created between the layers of paper. This was a particularly exciting discovery, as the challenge with albums is always how to allow expandable space for low-relief content. Initially, we designed this book with only four pages on each side of the triangular spine. Held upside down it really did resemble a daddy longlegs spider – thus the name for the book was coined.

COMPONENT	DIMENSIONS	QTY	PAPER
PAGES	6 x 14½ in. 14 x 37 cm	6	Cover-weight paper or cardstock: Japanese linen cardstock, 244g
COVERS	6 x 14½ in. 14 x 37 cm	2	Cover-weight paper or cardstock: Japanese linen cardstock, 244g
SPINE	6 x 6 in. 14 x 14 cm	1	Cover-weight paper or cardstock: Japanese linen cardstock, 244g

FINISHED DIMENSIONS:

6 x 8½ in. (14 x 22 cm)

TOOLS:

Self-healing cutting mat / Straight edge / Sharp knife / Clear plastic gridded ruler / Bone folder / Awl Pencil / Needle / Bulldog clips (4) Key stock / Double-sided tape / Barbour linen No 18/3 thread or similar

TECHNIQUES:

Using Key Stock and Box Corner Assembly, page 20

Preparing a Sewing Template, page 24

Sewing Folios, page 24

Measuring Devices: Paper Strips, page 18

NOTE

For this project, we recommend working with the key stock and box corner assembly. The key stock is used for scoring and is described in Techniques (page 20). As an alternative use a clear gridded ruler; or make your own scoring templates out of strips of medium-weight cardstock, at least 6 in. (14 cm) high and using the following dimensions for widths: ¼ in., ½ in., ¾ in., 1 in., 1¼ in., 1½ in. (1 cm, 1.5 cm, 2 cm, 2.5 cm, 3 cm, 3.5 cm).

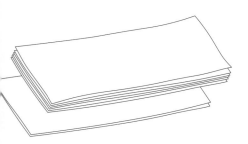

1. Cut eight pieces of paper to the given dimensions. The pages and covers are the same dimension. Set the covers aside.

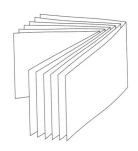

2. Fold the six pages in half to create folios.

3. Line up your key stock or scoring templates.

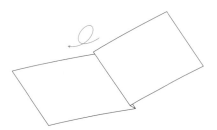

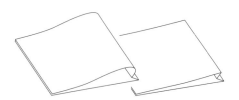

4. Start with the smallest unit of key stock and one folio. Line the key stock up with the fold and score against the key stock with a pointed bone folder or embossing stylus. Holding the key stock down tight, lift the top page up and score against the key stock from underneath.

5. Remove the key stock and fold the top page back on itself. Crease well. Turn the whole folio over to the left.

6. Bring the edge of the right page over to line up with the edge of the left page. Take care that the left edges remain aligned as you press down and crease well.

7. Repeat steps 4 through 6 with the remaining five pages, using consecutively larger key stock for each page.

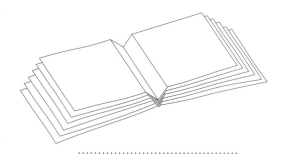

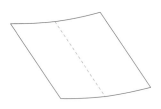

8. Nest the pages as shown, with the widest V on top.

9. Retrieve the spine piece and, with the wrong side facing you, fold it in half, with the direction of the grain running parallel to your fold.

10. Fold each side in half again and apply double-sided tape to the left outer section of the four.

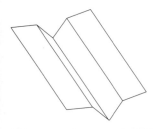

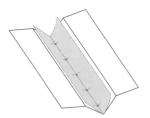

11. Reverse the two outer valley folds into mountain folds.

12. Prepare a sewing template with five holes (see page 24).

13. Nestle the template in the spine piece and pierce holes for sewing. Remove the sewing template.

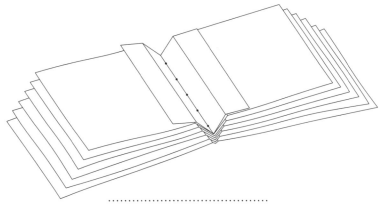

14. Nestle the spine piece in the pages.

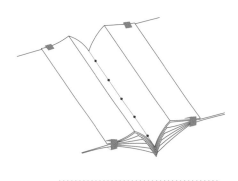

15. Secure the spine piece and pages with bulldog clips and pierce holes with an awl through all the pages at once.

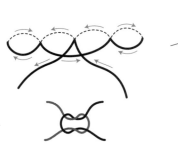

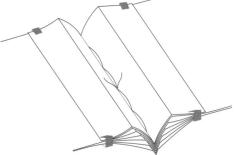

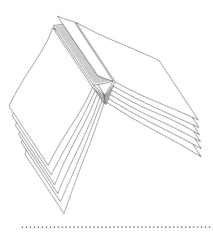

16. Thread a needle. Starting at the center hole, sew through all pages following the diagram shown here. Pulling the thread taut, secure the sewing with a square knot. Remove the bulldog clips.

17. Peel off the backing paper from the double-sided tape from one flap of the spine piece and adhere to the other flap, creating a hollow triangular spine.

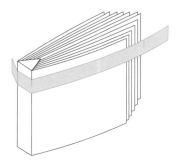

18. Use a paper strip to measure the thickness and width of the book.

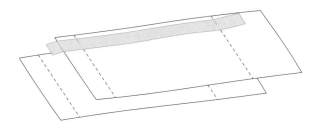

19. Retrieve the two cover pieces. Transfer the measurements from the paper strip to the two cover pieces, as shown, and score at the marks.

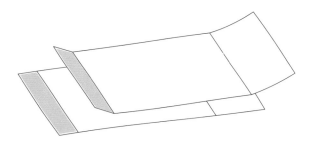

20. Apply double-sided tape to both spine sections.

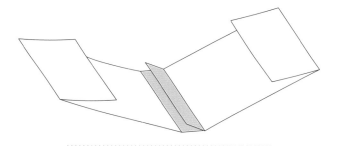

21. Fold and crease the score lines. Rotating one of the covers through 180 degrees, remove the backing paper from the bottom cover and attach the two spine sections to each other.

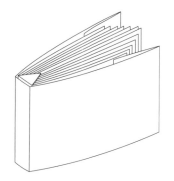

22. Removing the backing paper from what is now the inside of the cover, attach the spine to the book and turn in the cover extensions.

Fill the album with content of your choice. Take advantage of the fact that the layered spine and the resulting room between the pages allow for more three-dimensional material than you would normally be able to put in a book.

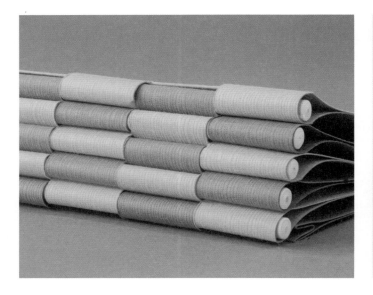

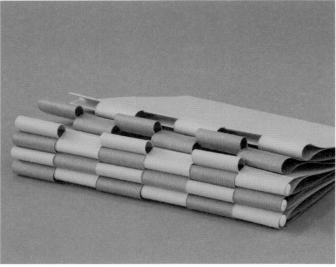

The requirements of a well functioning door and a well functioning book are the same – they need to open. The question that led to the development of this structure was simple: why couldn't a piece of hardware, such as a piano hinge, be adapted as a component for a book structure? After close observation, it was easy to translate the mechanism to another use and medium. This structure employs pages and covers that are identically cut. With the addition of a rod to connect, this structure is infinitely expandable. Experimenting with this model might lead you to ask, what other everyday objects can be translated into the medium of the book?

NOTES

Whatever rods or sticks or dowels you choose, they should be uniform in thickness. Simply measure the circumference and substitute that measurement for the one given.

Because the pages of this structure are interlocking, it is very important to keep the pages oriented top and bottom relative to one another.

COMPONENT	DIMENSIONS	QTY	PAPER
PAGES	6 x 8¾ in. 15 x 22 cm	6	Cover-weight paper or cardstock: Japanese linen cardstock, 244g
RODS	6 in. (15 cm) long, ¼ in. (6 mm) diameter, ¾ in. (2 cm) circumference	5	Lollipop sticks

FINISHED DIMENSIONS:
6 x 4⅜ in. (15 x 11 cm)

TOOLS:
Self-healing cutting mat / Straight edge / Sharp knife / Clear gridded ruler / Bone folder / Pencil / Lollipop sticks (rolled paper) – wooden dowels, plastic rods or pencils will also work / Key stock
Optional: Prepared cover boards, double-sided tape or PVA adhesive

TECHNIQUES:
Measuring Devices: Paper Strips, page 18

Using Key Stock and Box Corner Assembly, page 20

Centering a Spine, page 19

1. Measure the circumference of one rod with a strip of paper.

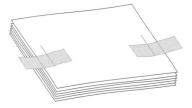

2. Transfer this measurement to each of the six pages with a pencil line, as shown.

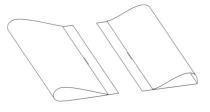

3. Center the spine fold: Take one page, bring the left side to the right pencil line, press down and crease. Bring the right side to the left pencil line, press down and crease. Repeat with the remaining five pages.

 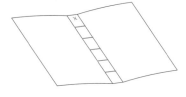 

4. Starting at the bottom edge of the page use a 1-in. (2.5-cm) key stock or clear gridded ruler to mark six sections with pencil lines. Take care to mark each page the same way. Mark the top of each page with an X to help keep the pages in this orientation.

5. Cut each page along the pencil lines, creating the segments of the piano hinge.

6. Roll the piano hinge of each page back and forth around a rod to form loops.

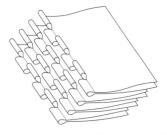 

7. On four of the pages, bend three loops to the left and three loops to the right.

8. The two remaining pages will become the front and back covers. Starting with the second loop on top of the left page and the first loop on top of the right page, invert three alternating loops on each page so that they have an opposite arrangement.

9. Starting with the cover on the left and one of the four pages in step 7, thread the first rod through the loops, engaging every other loop from each page. It may be helpful to use a rod coming from the opposite direction as you go to open up the loops.

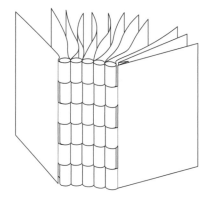

10. Adding pages, one at a time, and with rods, continue to interlock the loops. The remaining cover finishes the series. The cover folios can be taped or glued together to give a more rigid solution. Alternatively, hard covers may be adhered to the first and last pages using double-sided tape or PVA (see Use of Adhesive when Preparing Stiff Covers, page 25).

A single rod engineers the opening and closing of pages of this variation of the piano hinge album. An important distinction between this structure and the previously described piano hinge is an accordion spine to which individual folios are attached. Like the Piano Hinge, this structure is able to accommodate photographs, prints or drawings. Window cut-outs are made to the pages to which Mylar inserts filled with content such as collage material and stencils can be attached. The Mylar allows light to pass through the pages, creating shadows and reflections similar to an early cinematic device.

COMPONENT	DIMENSIONS	QTY	PAPER
ACCORDION	6 x 12 in. 15 x 32 cm	1	Text-weight paper: Elephant hide paper, 110 gsm
PAGES	6 x 17 in. 15 x 44 cm	4	Cover-weight paper: French Speckletone 80C
POCKETS	4½ x 14 in. 13 x 40 cm	4	Mylar
COVERS	6 x 17½ in. 15 x 46 cm	2	Cover-weight paper or cardstock: Japanese linen cardstock, 244g
ROD	6 in. (15 cm) long, ¼ in. (6 mm) diameter, ¾ in. (2 cm) circumference	1	Lollipop stick

FINISHED DIMENSIONS:
6 x 9 in. (15 x 23 cm)

TECHNIQUES:
Folding an Accordion 2–4–8, pages 30–32

Dividing into an Odd Number of Sections, page 20

TOOLS:
Self-healing cutting mat / Straight edge / Ruler / Sharp knife / Bone folder / Pencil / Double-sided tape / Lollipop stick, dowel, plastic rod or a round pencil / Content for Mylar pockets, such as cut-outs that will produce shadows / Paper clips

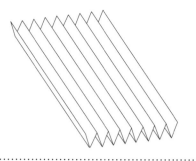

1. Fold a 16-section accordion.

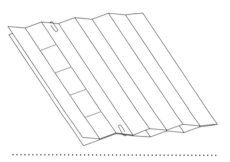

2. Open the accordion and fold it in half. Paper clip it together. Divide and mark the second and fifteenth sections into five equal parts. Make a horizontal cut at each mark through both layers, taking care to line them up exactly.

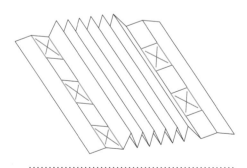

3. Open the accordion and complete the cutting as shown, removing fully the pieces marked with an X.

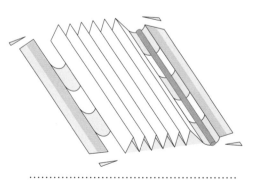

4. Gently round the second and fifteenth sections with the help of the stick. Apply double-sided tape to the first and last sections, placing it close to the folded edges. Trim off small triangles from the top and bottom of these sections.

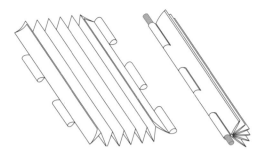

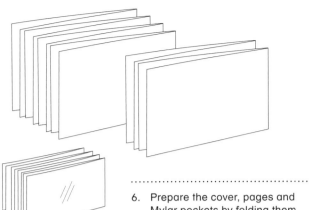

5. Adhere the two sections on either side of the cut-outs, creating loops. Compress the accordion, lining up the loops, and thread the stick through the loops.

6. Prepare the cover, pages and Mylar pockets by folding them all in half widthwise.

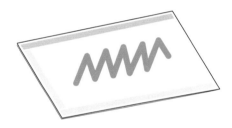

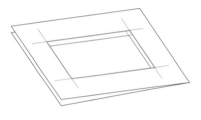

7. Apply double-sided tape to the three unfolded edges of the four Mylar pockets.

8. Enclose your content, peel off the backing paper from the tape and tape the sides shut. Apply one additional strip of tape along the top edge of the Mylar pocket.

9. Cut out windows in the four pages, leaving 1¼-in. (3-cm) borders all around.

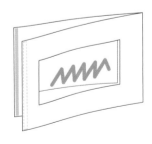

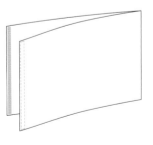

10. Peel the backing paper off the tape on the top edge of the Mylar pockets and adhere to the inside of one side of the pages. Apply double-sided tape to the insides of the page along the short unfolded edges, as shown.

11. Apply double-sided tape to the insides of the covers, along the short unfolded edges.

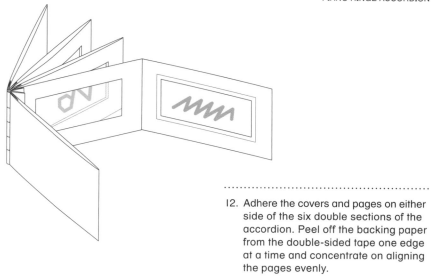

12. Adhere the covers and pages on either side of the six double sections of the accordion. Peel off the backing paper from the double-sided tape one edge at a time and concentrate on aligning the pages evenly.

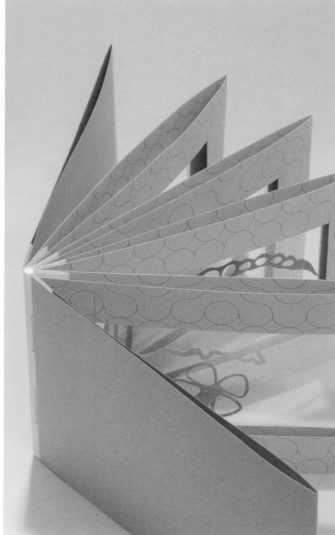

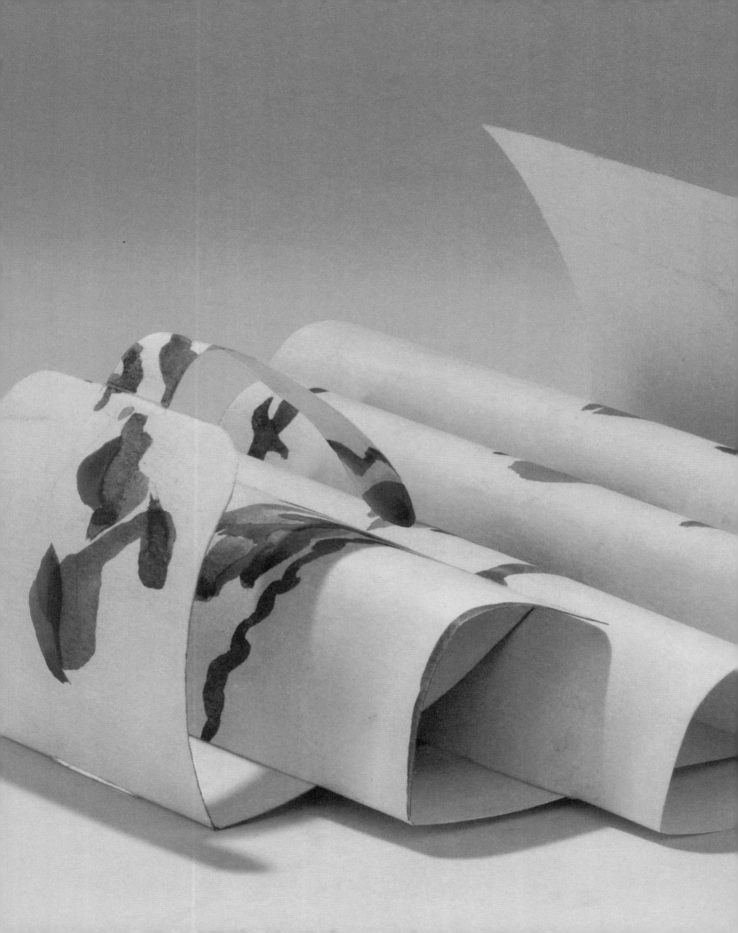

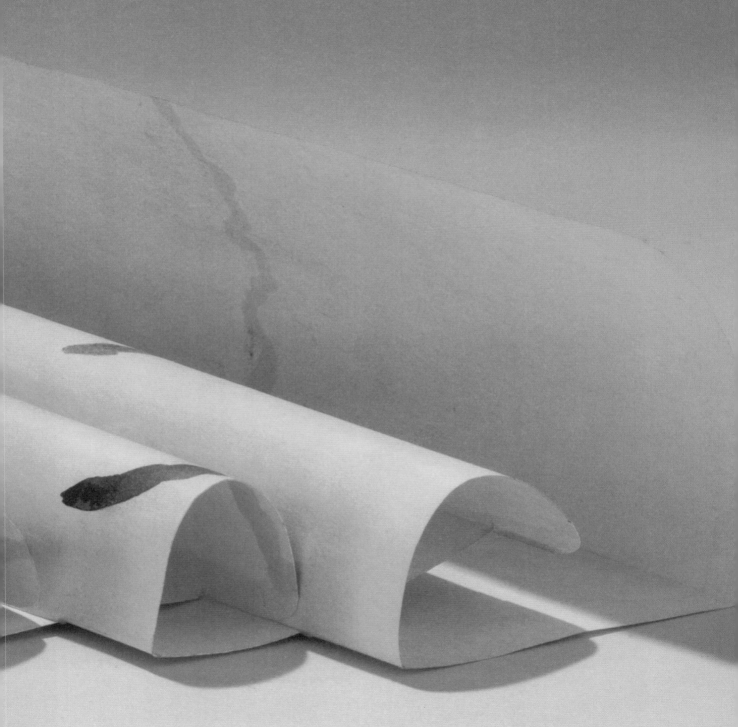

5
Enclosures

Enclosures

A book or an object is protected and often enhanced when partnered with a customized enclosure. Enclosures have multiple functions – they heighten suspense, keep fragile items safe and present a disparate series of objects as a unified whole. An enclosure may become an essential part of a whole, like a vestibule that leads into an inner chamber or a cabinet of treasures. You will have encountered several projects in this book that do not require traditional, attached covers. Made out of stiff paper, they function quite well on their own or are designed to be sculptural objects, much more alive in their three-dimensional form than hidden away between covers. Wrappers, slipcases and envelopes are an ideal way to house these types of structures. Like a hermit crab, they can be detached from their shell but nonetheless have a place for safekeeping. In this chapter we present a selection of enclosures inspired by a variety of sources including library conservation, trade manuals, a sewing machine parts box, and even a wrapper from our school days! They are highly versatile by nature and can be easily modified to fit many of the projects in the previous chapters to make unique pairings.

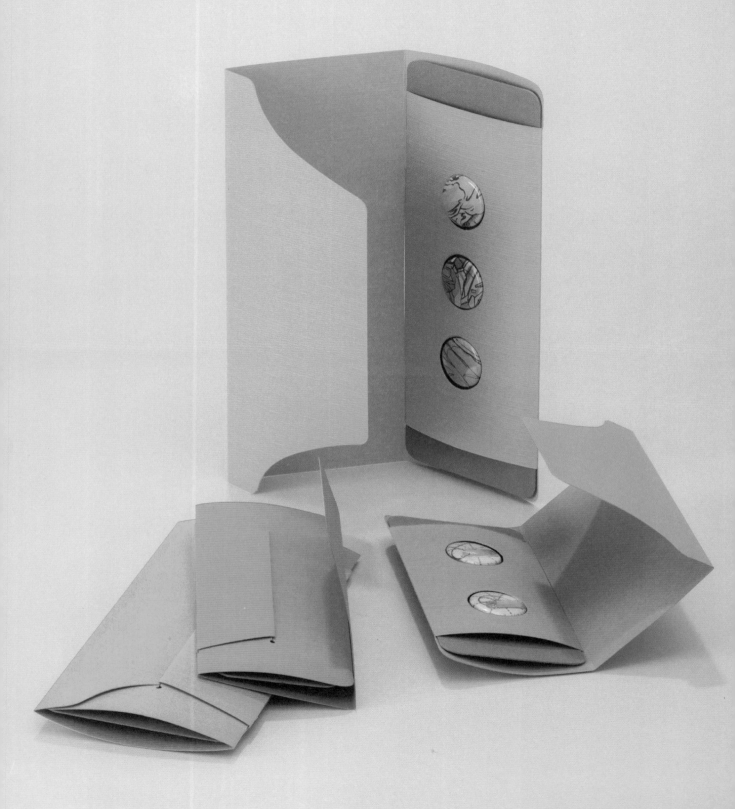

The Button Pouch grew out of an encounter with an old trade manual. There we found a detail of a holding device for a ruler, achieved by threading a strip of paper through a slot in a fold and fastening it underneath. The flexible nature of this hinging mechanism, the idea of using a strip of paper as its own thread, stuck with us. We enlarged upon this technique to create the Button Pouch which, due to its rolling fold and lozenge shape, accommodates three-dimensional items. A further investigation led us to develop the Sling Fold (pages 156–61).

NOTE

Before you begin this project, find the object (or objects) you wish to enclose in the pouch. It should be a low-relief object such as a button.

COMPONENT	DIMENSIONS	QTY	PAPER
RECTANGLE	6 x 15 in. <u>15</u> x 40 cm	I	Cover-weight paper or cardstock: Japanese linen cardstock, 244g
INSERT	<u>5¾</u> x 2⅞ in. <u>14.5</u> x 7.7 cm	I	Cardstock or thin board
TEMPLATE	Measure to match insert	I	Cardstock: Japanese linen cardstock, 244g

FINISHED DIMENSIONS:
6 x 3 in. (15 x 8 cm)

TOOLS:
Self-healing cutting mat / Straight edge / Sharp knife / Paper cutter (optional) / Awl / Scissors / Bone folder / Pencil / Corner rounder (optional)

TECHNIQUES:
Rolling Folds, page 23

Rounding Corners, page 21

Making Non-Tear Slits with Anchor Holes, page 21

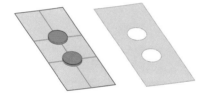

1. Attach the object to the insert card as you would like it to appear in the pouch. Create an identical template with a cut-out to display the object.

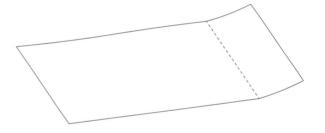

2. With the wrong side of your paper facing you, measure and make the first fold at 3 in. (8 cm) from the right-hand side, creating the first section. Crease well.

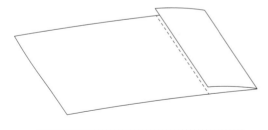

3. Using the rolling method of score and crease, create the next section.

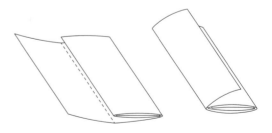

4. Repeat twice more. All folds are valley folds and you should have five sections.

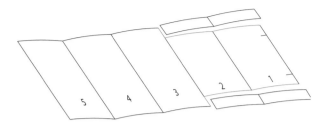

5. Unfold at this juncture, and number the five sections lightly with a pencil on the bottom on both sides. Cut a ¾-in. (2-cm) strip from the head and tail of sections 1 and 2.

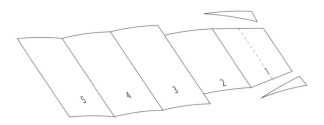

6. Measure down ¾ in. (2 cm) from the head and tail of section 1 and remove triangular pieces, as shown. Fold section 1 in half, crease and then unfold.

7. Roll section 1 onto section 2 and then roll both onto section 3.

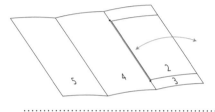

8. Mark with a pencil where section 2 meets the fold. Unfold, punch holes and cut a slot connecting these two marks. It should be just to the right of the valley fold.

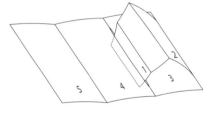

9. Thread section 1 into the slot just created. Pull through to the other side.

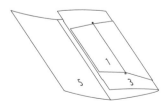

10. Turn section 3 along with section 1. Mark the head and tail of the midway fold of section 1 onto section 3 with a pencil.

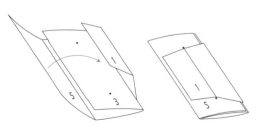

11. Lift section 1, bring section 5 over and position it under section 1. Mark the head and tail of the midway fold of section 1 onto section 5 with a pencil.

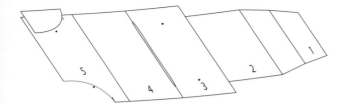

12. Unfold the entire piece and flip it over so that the mountain folds are facing up. You should see your pencil marks. Mark ¾ in. (2 cm) up from the fold at the head and tail of section 5. Make a curved cut just inside the two pencil marks to create a pleasing shape. Use the cut-out of one corner to trace the other for symmetry.

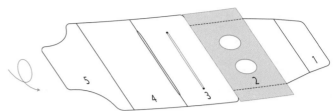

13. Punch holes at the marks on section 3 and cut a slot between them. Retrieve the template and, centering it on section 2, cut out the area where your content will be displayed. Round or ease the corners as shown with corner rounder or by hand (optional).

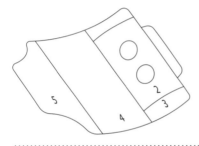

14. Flip the pouch over so that the valley folds are facing up. Thread section 1 through the slot at the fold.

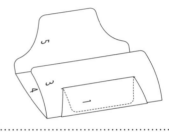

15. Turning the pouch as shown, thread section 1 into the midway slot.

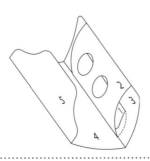

16. Gently coax the fore-edge of section 1 to fold downward, on itself, inside the pouch. This is a little tricky, but will create a distinct edge for the end flap of section 5 to tuck into.

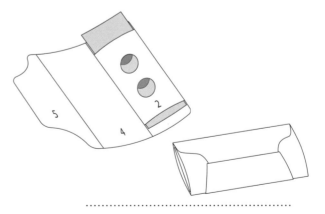

17. Slide the card insert in between panels 2 and 3. Bring flap 5 around to tuck into the opening at section 3.

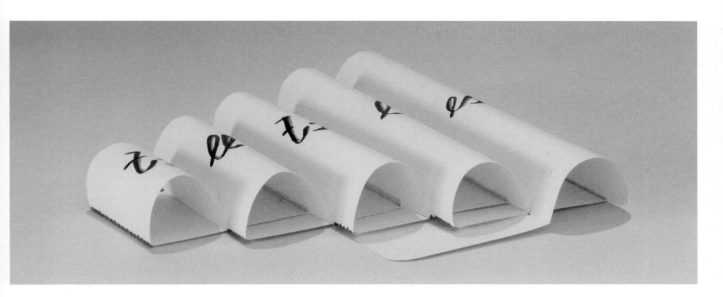

The Sling Fold's appearance can be deceiving at first. It can stand upright like a traditional book structure or it can be uncoiled and sprung open to reveal the surfaces beneath its pages. Its structure is achieved by threading and looping a single strip of paper through a succession of slits. At first this technique seems rather convoluted and, as far as we know, it is unrelated to any traditional binding styles. However we discovered that, due to its unconventional operating system, the Sling Fold can serve as a vehicle for the juxtaposition of text and images.

NOTE
A thin but strong paper is ideal for this project and so we include Tyvek in the list of papers. Tyvek folds and rolls well, cuts easily and, most importantly, does not tear – three critical conditions for this project. For sources, see page 13.

COMPONENT	DIMENSIONS	QTY	PAPER
ACCORDION	9 x 30 in. 23 x 75 cm	1	Text-weight paper: Elephant hide paper, 110 gsm, Tyvek

FINISHED DIMENSIONS:
9 x 3 in. (23 x 7.5 cm)

TOOLS:
Self-healing cutting mat
Straight edge / Ruler / Sharp
knife / Bone folder / Awl / Pencil
Optional: Key stock – ¾ in. (2 cm)
Corner rounder

TECHNIQUES:
Folding an Accordion 2–4–8,
pages 30–32

Rounding Corners and Thumb
Notches, page 21

Making Non-Tear Slits with Anchor
Holes, page 21

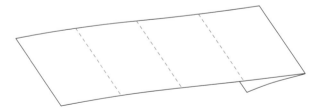

1. Mark 6 in. (15 cm) from the right-hand edge of your strip and fold this portion under. Fold the remaining portion into four equal parts.

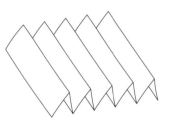

2. Including the fifth portion from step 1, fold all into a ten-section accordion with five mountain folds facing you.

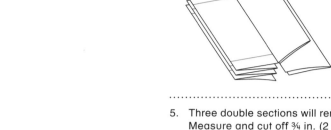

3. Collapse into a stack and turn one double section over to your right. A stack of four double sections will remain to your left. Measure and cut off ¾ in. (2 cm) along the head and tail of the stack using the key stock or a ruler.

5. Three double sections will remain. Measure and cut off ¾ in. (2 cm) from the head and tail of the stack and turn the top double section over to your right.

4. Turn the top double section over to your right.

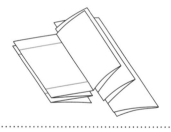

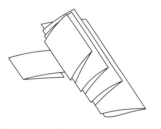

6. Repeat this process twice more.

7. When you arrive at the last double section, unfold the strip.

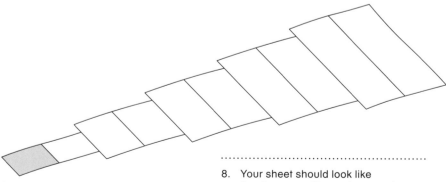

8. Your sheet should look like the diagram, with evenly spaced stepped-down cut-aways. The smallest section on the end is declared the leader, so mark it in some way on both sides.

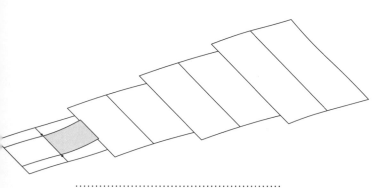

9. Fold the first two sections on the left over to the right. Line up the center fold with the center fold underneath and make marks at both ends of the shorter fold using an awl.

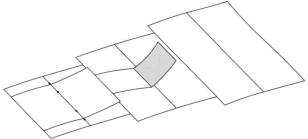

10. Move the leader another two sections to the right and again mark the top and bottom of the shorter fold.

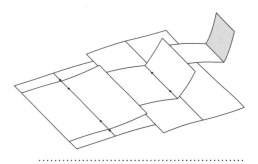

11. Continue this process.

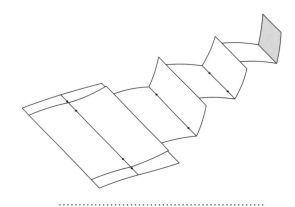

12. All the center folds have been marked except for the leader's.

13. Open the strip up. Check the diagram and punch small holes at the marks or enlarge the awl pricks slightly. Cut slits between the holes.

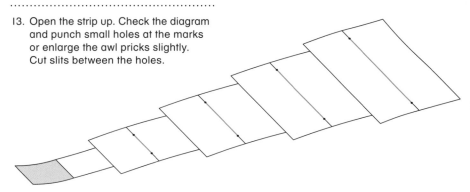

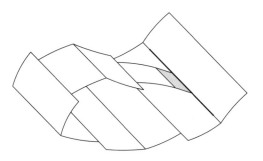

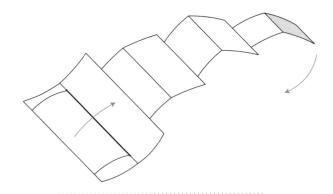

....

14. Now begin the threading. Bring the leader across and thread it through the longest slit to your right.

....

15. Guide all sections through the slit, moving them to the right until they come to a stop as shown in the diagram, creating a sling fold. Turn the sling fold over from left to right and bring the leader back around to the left.

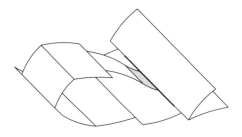

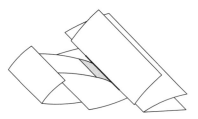

....

16. Guide the leader through the next-longest slit to the right until it comes to a stop. Turn that sling fold over to the right.

....

17. Repeat, each time turning the newest sling fold to the right and threading the leader through the next-longest slit.

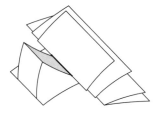

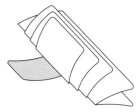

....

18. Repeat one more time.

....

19. We rounded the corners on our model at this point, but that is entirely optional.

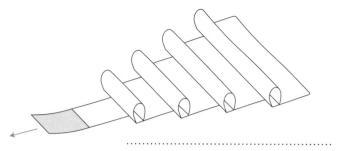

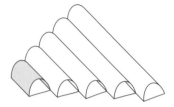

20. Gently pull on the leader to roll up the sections for a special effect.

21. By coaxing the rolls and tucking the leader in at the end, a rhythm of arches is created.

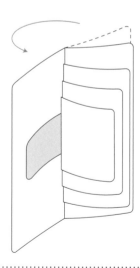

22. In its flat state, bring the last section of the sling fold to the front to serve as the cover. As you stand this book up, you'll notice a built-in curvature to the pages.

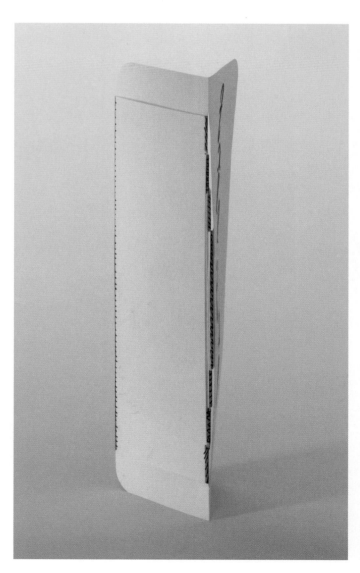

We love the in-between realm that the Telescoping Ziggurat occupies – it's neither a scroll nor an accordion. This structure is really less of a book and more of a toy – a stimulating and curious object whose inherent mathematical quality mesmerizes as it spirals inward and outward. Quite simple to make, it is also a hybrid of techniques we've described thus far – the rolling fold (page 23) and Folding an Accordion (Chapter 1). Additional lengths of paper can be added and the height can easily be modified. This structure is completely open ended and that, we believe, is the beauty of it.

COMPONENT	DIMENSIONS	QTY	PAPER
STRIPS	3½ x 36½ in. 9 x 92 cm	2	Medium-weight paper on a roll or cover-weight paper: Elephant hide paper, 190 gsm; Japanese linen cardstock, 244g

FINISHED DIMENSIONS:
3½ x 36½ in. (9 x 92 cm)

TOOLS:
Self-healing cutting mat / Straight edge / Ruler / Sharp knife / Bone folder / Pencil / Spacer, ¼-in. (5-mm) key stock or similar device / Double-sided tape

TECHNIQUES:
Folding an Accordion 2–4–8, pages 30–32

Rolling Folds, page 23

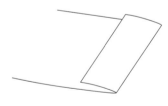

1. Starting at the right-hand edge of the first strip, fold over 1 in. (2.5 cm) to the left.

2. Line your ¼-in. (5-mm) spacer up with the edge of the portion you just brought over and, with your bone folder, score against the spacer.

3. Remove the spacer, lift up the right portion and bring it over to lie flat on the strip. Crease well.

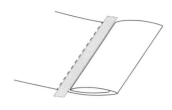

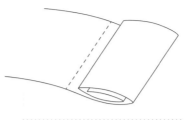

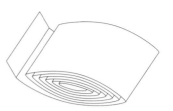

4. Line your spacer up with the fold again and repeat steps 2 and 3.

5. Continue this action.

6. When the strip is used up, you will have a small extra portion at the left-hand end. This serves to attach the next strip. Turn the strip over so that your folds become mountain folds.

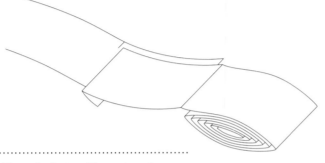

7. Place the last and largest section on the second strip and transfer the measurement to the second strip.

8. To the second strip, add the width of the spacer, score and make your first fold by bringing the portion over to the left. Set the second strip aside.

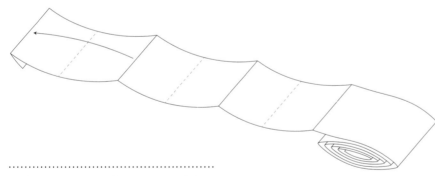

9. Return to strip 1. Starting at the left, bring mountain fold to mountain fold, lining them up and creasing them well.

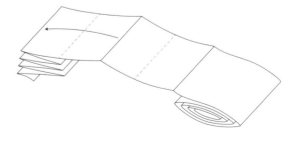

10. Continue this folding process until the whole strip is folded and the narrowest portion lies on top.

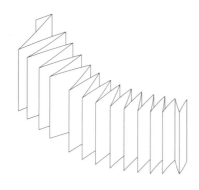

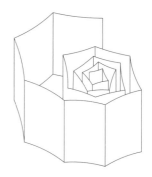

11. Stand the strip up as an accordion. Mountain and valley folds alternate.

12. Turn all the valley folds into mountain folds.

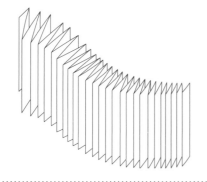

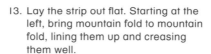

13. Lay the strip out flat. Starting at the left, bring mountain fold to mountain fold, lining them up and creasing them well.

14. Stand the strip up again as an accordion. Mountain and valley folds alternate, as in step 11, but now you have twice as many folds. Turn all the valley folds into mountain folds.

16. Retrieve the second strip. Follow the directions in steps 2 through 6, starting with the portion you measured and folded over in step 7. Once you have completed the valley folds, repeat steps 9 through 14. Attach the second strip to the extra portion of the first strip with double-sided tape and repeat step 15.

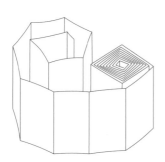

15. Starting with the first narrow section, roll four mountain folds into a square. Continue to follow this pattern as the square grows in size to form the Telescoping Ziggurat.

The Star Box is inspired by old Singer sewing-machine parts boxes that roll up in a similar fashion. The box is divided into four triangular compartments and in the process of rolling the box up, a star shape emerges, hence its name. The display area of the Star Box is reminiscent of a set of open drawers lined up next to each other, each containing an array of things visible all at once.

COMPONENT	DIMENSIONS	QTY	PAPER
RECTANGLE	7½ x 11¾ in. 19 x 31.5 cm	1	Cover-weight paper or cardstock: French Dur-O-Tone 80C Elephant hide paper, 190 gsm
STRIPS	See instructions before cutting	3	

FINISHED DIMENSIONS:
6 x 1½ x 1½ in. (16 x 4 x 4 cm)

TOOLS:
Self-healing cutting mat / Straight edge / Ruler / Sharp knife / Bone folder / Awl / Pencil / PVA adhesive / Double-sided tape / Key stock (optional)

TECHNIQUE:
Using Key Stock and Box Corner Assembly, page 20

Cutting Angles, Darts and Slivers, page 21

Rounding Corners and Thumb Notches, page 21

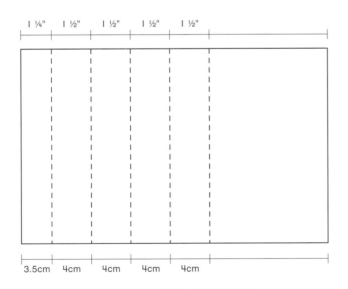

1. Using the dimensions provided, mark and score all the fold lines with a ruler or key stock.

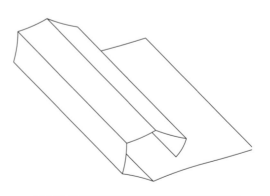

2. Crease into valley folds. Flatten the piece.

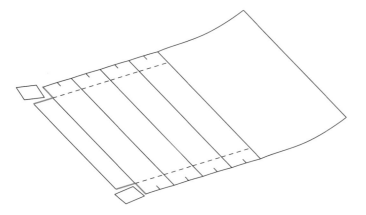

3. Mark and score ¾ in. (2 cm) up and down from the head and tail and only between the folds. Cut out the corner pieces at the left. Mark the middle of each of the four equal sections.

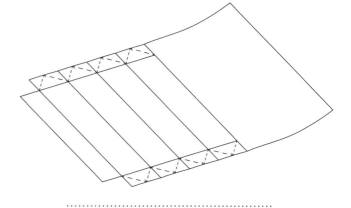

4. Score diagonally in both directions from the marks to the ¾-in. (2-cm) score lines.

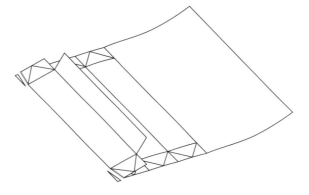

5. Bring the four equal sections one by one over to the right and cut a thin dart off at their head and tail. Repeat four times.

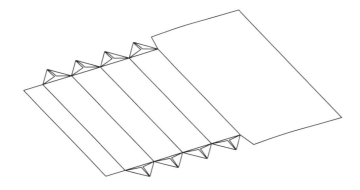

6. Flatten the piece and turn the small scored triangles in, creasing them well.

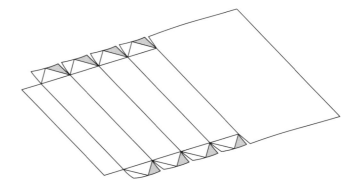

7. Lift the triangles and apply PVA adhesive to the triangles shown as shaded...

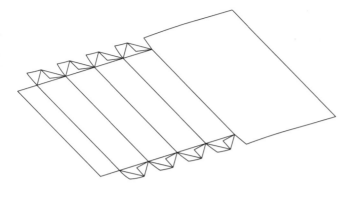

8. ...and glue them down.

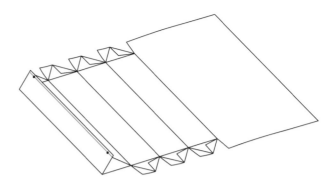

9. Stand the first pair of triangles up. Align the first section with the side of the triangles and make a mark to establish the exact height of this partition. Trim off the excess.

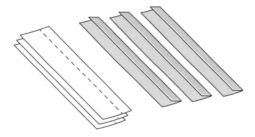

10. Cut three strips from the same paper to the height and width of the partition you just measured, plus additional width to add double-sided tape. Score, crease and apply double-sided tape to the narrower portion.

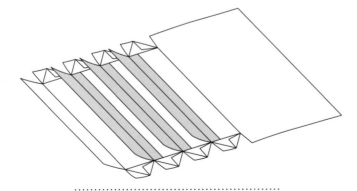

11. Adhere the folded strips flush with the left folds of the equal sections 2, 3 and 4 to create partitions. The partition for section 1 is the smaller section to the far left.

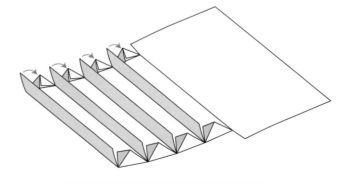

12. Stand the partitions up. Apply adhesive to the free small triangles and adhere them to the partitions.

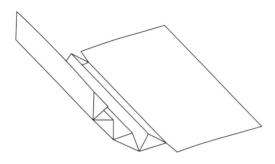

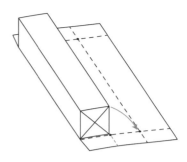

13. Roll the box over onto the part reserved for the lid.

14. As you roll the box, mark with an awl, score and crease the depth, width and height of the lid. For a better fit of the lid, allow a little extra space between the box walls and the marks.

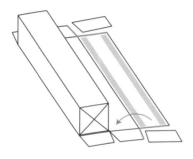

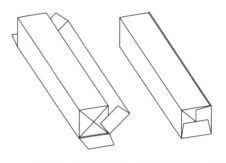

15. Cut darts at the head and tail, between the first and second lid sections, to create tabs. Cut and remove the two rectangles from the third section and apply double-sided tape, as shown. Fold over and adhere to the second lid section.

16. Fold the lid around the box. Use adhesive (or tape) to adhere the tabs.

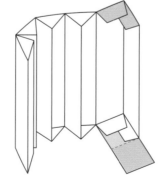

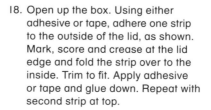

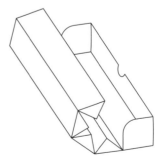

17. Cut two strips 1½ x 3¼ in. (4 x 8.5 cm).

18. Open up the box. Using either adhesive or tape, adhere one strip to the outside of the lid, as shown. Mark, score and crease at the lid edge and fold the strip over to the inside. Trim to fit. Apply adhesive or tape and glue down. Repeat with second strip at top.

19. Cut a thumb notch and round the corners of the lid. Fill with a collection needing a home.

The ubiquitous school-book wrapper is known throughout the world. A non-adhesive, removable and replaceable wrapper, it can be made out of relatively thin paper. Because of its double thickness and folded edges, it is surprisingly resilient and its simplicity makes it an enduring design. We present instructions for the original and then modify this old friend by lengthening the sheet of paper, wrapping it around the entire book and ending in a tab that tucks neatly into an integrated pleat. Both versions can be used for accordions, many of the blizzards, fishbone and tree folds. A slight variation appears in the Triangular Book (pages 100–103) and is described there.

COMPONENT	DIMENSIONS	QTY	PAPER
RECTANGLE	See instructions before cutting	I	Paper on a roll

FINISHED DIMENSIONS:
Variable

TOOLS:
Self-healing cutting mat / Straight edge / Sharp knife / Paper cutter (optional) / Scissors / Bone folder Pencil

TECHNIQUES:
Centering a Spine, page 19

Measuring with Templates, page 19

Knife Pleats and Box Pleats, page 23

Inside Reverse Fold, page 22

School-Book Wrapper

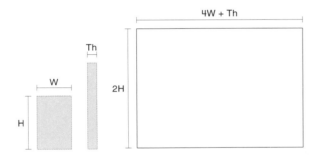

1. To lay out the wrapper, cut two templates – one representing the height and width of your book, the other one the thickness of the spine. Using the templates, cut a sheet of paper following the equations given.

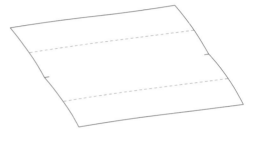

2. Mark the center of the short ends and fold the long sides up and down to meet at the center.

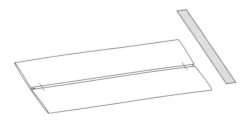

3. Using the spine template, transfer the thickness of the spine to both ends of the wrapper piece.

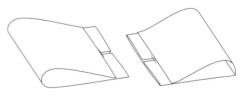

4. Fold the left side over to the right mark and crease. Fold the right side over to the left mark and crease. A spine thickness is created at the center.

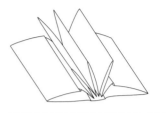

5. A spine thickness is centered in the wrapper.

6. Fold the covers over to line up with the spine folds and crease well at the fore-edge.

7. Insert the first and last pages or cards attached to hinges into the covers.

School-Book Wrapper with Pleat

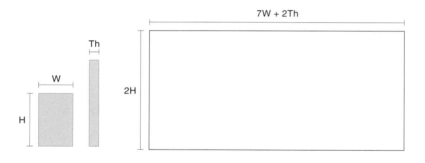

1. To lay out the wrapper, cut two templates – one representing the height and width of your book, the other the thickness of the spine. Using the templates, cut a sheet of paper following the equations given.

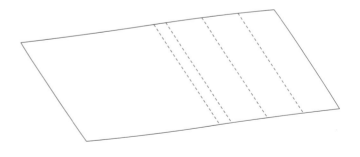

2. Using the templates again, measure, mark and score the first four folds using both templates (three widths and one spine thickness).

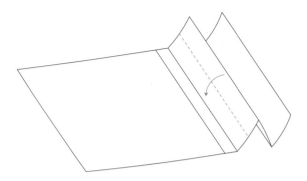

3. Bring the second fold over to meet the third fold, creating a pleat.

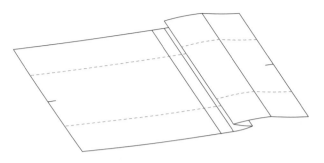

4. Mark the center of the two short ends and fold the long sides up and down to meet at the center.

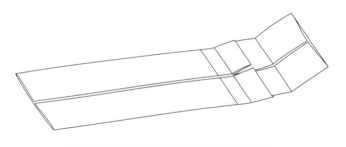

5. Crease well.

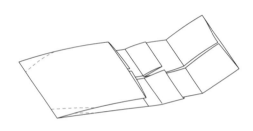

6. Bring the left side over to the first spine fold. Make diagonal folds at the corners and inside reverse fold.

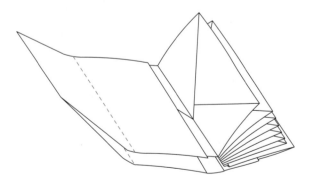

7. Insert the first and last pages of the book into the cavities in the cover. Making a soft fold, wrap the flap around the fore-edge of the book and tuck it into the pleat.

The partial slipcase, a non-adhesive flexible container folded from a single sheet of paper, can stand on its own as a temporary holding device for a work in progress. It is also the inner component of the two-part slipcase, which features reinforced partial spine walls and full sides that have a tendency to slightly flare out, allowing for easy removal of materials.

     The full slipcase is, so to speak, the lid for the partial one. It requires a larger sheet of paper due to its full spine height and to compensate for the perfect fit when absorbing the partial slipcase. Because of their flexible nature, the two slipcases can be easily separated and pulled apart. Both work well when folded from a paper such as Japanese Momi, a soft, textured paper with a cushioned feel to it. You can also use found paper such as a brown paper bag, crumple it and then flatten it. This technique yields a similar effect.

NOTE

As an example, we have sized this slipcase to accommodate the Blizzard Book, pages 70–73.

FINISHED DIMENSIONS:
Variable

TOOLS:
Self-healing cutting mat / Straight edge / Ruler / Sharp knife / Paper cutter (optional) / Awl / Scissors / Bone folder / Pencil / Double-sided tape

TECHNIQUES:
Measuring Devices: Paper Strips and Templates, pages 18–19

Centering a Spine, page 19

COMPONENT	DIMENSIONS	QTY	PAPER
RECTANGLE	See instructions before cutting	1	Text-weight paper: Japanese Momi paper, 90G
TEMPLATES	See instructions before cutting	2	Cover-weight paper or cardstock

Slipcase with Partial Sides

1. Start with your contents. With a ruler or a strip of paper, measure the height (H), width (W) and thickness (Th) of your contents. If your contents are made up of several structures, treat them as a block. Make a table noting these measurements.

	in	cm
W	2"	5.5
H	3⅝	9
Th	⅝	1.7

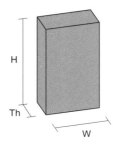

2. Using the dimensions, make two templates following the equations provided. Label them template 1 (H x W) and template 2, the thickness strip.

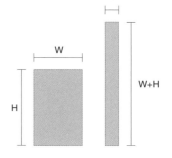

3. Prepare a large sheet, wrong side up, with the grain running vertically. Make a pencil line showing the grain direction. This will be helpful in orienting the paper. Using the templates, cut the paper to size according to the equations given.

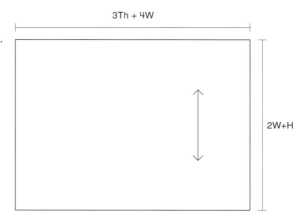

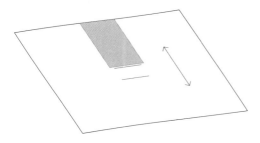

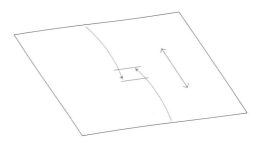

4. With the paper oriented so that the grain direction arrow is vertical, take template I, line it up at the top edge of the paper and mark the height. Repeat at the bottom edge.

5. These marks do not show the location of folds! They are simply guides to help position the height in the center of the paper. Take note of the arrows and proceed to the next step.

6. Bring the top edge down to the lower mark...

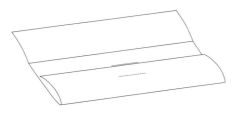

7. ...and the lower edge to the upper mark, creasing both well.

8. Open up and fold the top and bottom sections in half. Crease well.

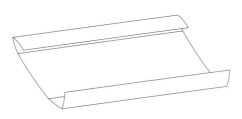

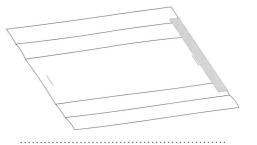

9. A section now appears in the center of the sheet that represents the height of the book.

10. Using template 2, mark the thickness at the right and left sides of the sheet.

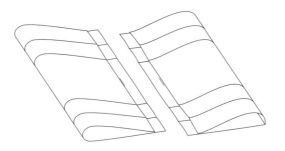

....

11. Bring the left side over to the right
mark and the right side over to the
left mark, creasing both well.

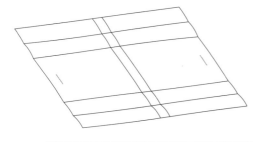

....

12. A section now appears in the center
of the sheet that represents the spine
thickness of the book.

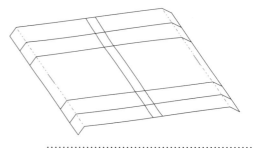

....

13. Make two folds at the right and left
sides, along the marks you made with
template 2.

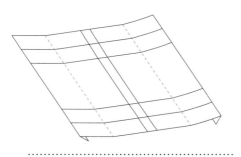

....

14. Turn these folds under and crease well.

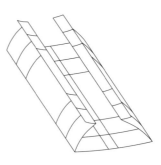

....

15. Bring the folded edges at right and left
to the corresponding folds at the spine.

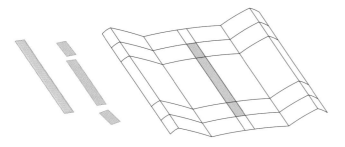

16. To add spine reinforcement, apply double-sided tape to template 2 and cut the strip to match the locations shown, trimming if necessary. Attach.

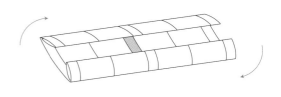

17. Fold the two long sides over, rolling them as you go. Rotate the piece to a vertical position.

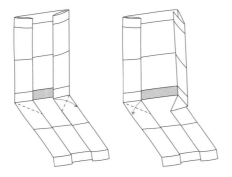

18. Bring one of the smaller spine sections forward and out to align with the edge of the case, creating an inside corner. Repeat on the other side. Using a small triangle to pre-score a diagonal crease in the direction shown may be helpful the first time.

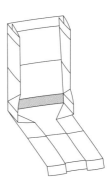

19. Flip the piece around and repeat this process on the other side.

20. Turn the two side walls inward at the folds. The narrow portions will nestle between the spine folds.

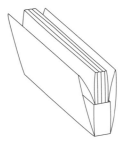

21. Insert the contents into the partial slipcase. Proceed to the Slipcase with Full Sides.

Slipcase with Full Sides

This slipcase with full sides will enclose the partial side slipcase, acting like the well-fitting cover of a box. Be aware that the base sheet for this piece is a different proportion than the partial side slipcase. It is larger and more vertical in the orientation when starting out.

	in	cm
W	2¼"	5.5
H	3⅝	9
Th	⅝	1.7

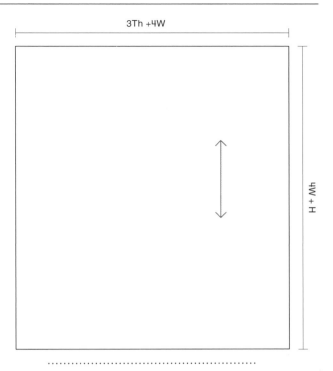

1. With a ruler or a strip of paper, measure the height (H), width (W) and thickness (Th) of your content. In this case, your content is the Slipcase with Partial Sides. Make a table noting these measurements. Cut two templates, 1 and 2, following the equations provided.

2. Prepare a large sheet, wrong side up, with the grain running vertically. Make a pencil line showing the grain direction. This will be helpful in orienting the paper. Using the templates, cut the paper to size according to the equations given.

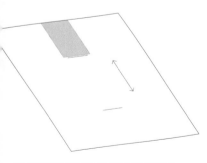

3. With the paper oriented so that the grain direction arrow is vertical, take template 1, line it up at the top edge of the paper and mark the height. Repeat at the bottom edge.

4. Bring the top edge down to the lower mark...

5. ...and the lower edge to the upper mark, creasing both well.

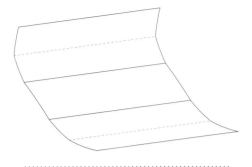

6. Open up and fold the top and bottom sections in half. Crease well.

7. A section now appears in the center of the sheet that represents the height of the slipcase with partial sides.

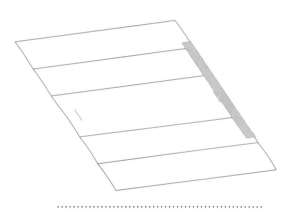

8. Using template 2, mark the thickness at the right and left sides of the sheet.

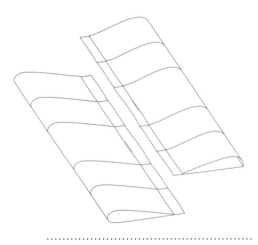

9. Bring the left side over to the right mark and the right side over to the left mark, creasing both well.

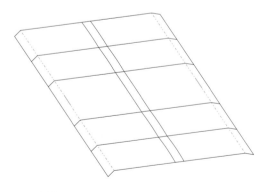

10. A section now appears in the center of the sheet that represents the spine thickness of the Slipcase with Partial Sides. Make two folds at the right and left sides, along the marks you made with template 2.

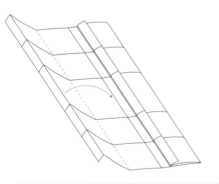

11. Turn these folds under, crease well and bring the folded edges at the right and left to the corresponding folds at the spine.

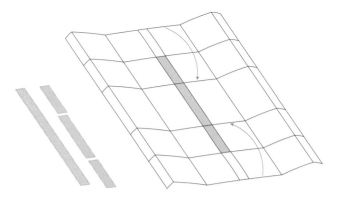

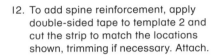

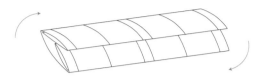

12. To add spine reinforcement, apply double-sided tape to template 2 and cut the strip to match the locations shown, trimming if necessary. Attach.

13. Fold the two short sides over, rolling them as you go. They will overlap. Rotate the piece to a vertical position.

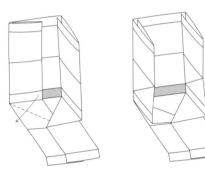

14. Bring one of the smaller spine sections forward and out to align with the edge of the case, creating an inside corner. Repeat on the other side. Using a small triangle to pre-score a diagonal crease in the direction shown may be helpful the first time. Flip the piece around and repeat this process on the other side.

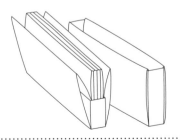

15. Turn the two side walls inward at the folds. The narrow portions will nestle between the spine folds.

16. Insert the Slipcase with Partial Sides and you have a complete set.

36 Self-Closing Wrapper

The Self-Closing Wrapper has utilitarian roots. Designed as a temporary holding device for library conservation purposes, it is simple to make and can hold one or several items that are awaiting rebinding or are too fragile to stand alone on a library shelf. However, we find it to be remarkably versatile and have re-sized it to become a handsome container for a series of three small books in Chapter 3 – the Four-Way Map Fold, the Triangular Book, and the Franklin Fold. Customize the self-closing wrapper to the size of a book you already own or use with any of the structures described in these chapters.

COMPONENT	DIMENSIONS	QTY	PAPER
RECTANGLE	5½ x 10 in. 14 x 27 cm See instructions before cutting	1	Cover-weight paper or cardstock: Japanese linen cardstock, 244g
RECTANGLE	3 x 12½ in. 7.5 x 34 cm See instructions before cutting	1	Cover-weight paper or cardstock: Japanese linen cardstock, 244g

FINISHED DIMENSIONS:
5½ x 3 x ¾ in. (14 x 7.5 x 2 cm)

TOOLS:
Self-healing cutting mat / Straight edge / Ruler / Sharp knife / Paper cutter (optional) / Awl / Scissors / Bone folder / Pencil / Gouge to cut notch (optional) / Double-sided tape

TECHNIQUES:
Rounding Corners and Thumb Notches, page 21

Marking with an Awl, page 18

Measuring Devices: Paper Strip, page 18

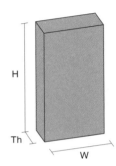

	in.	cm
W	3"	7.5
H	5½	14
Th	¾	2.8

1. With a ruler or a strip of paper, measure the height (H), width (W) and thickness (Th) of your contents. If your contents are made up of several structures, treat them as a block. Make a table noting these measurements.

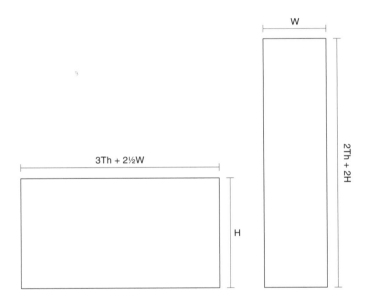

2. We provide dimensions for this wrapper, but you can follow these equations to cut paper to fit any content of your choice.

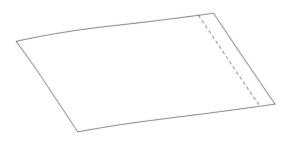

3. Transfer the thickness (Th) measurement to the short edge of the horizontal piece, score and crease well.

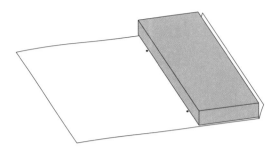

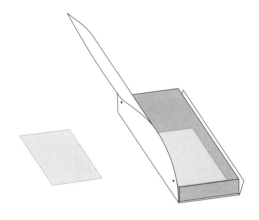

4. Stand this portion up, place your content against it and mark the width with an awl. Remove the content, score between the awl marks and crease.

5. Create a double-thickness spacer made from the same material as the wrapper. Replace the content, position the spacer on top flush with the left flap standing up and mark the thickness with an awl. Remove the content, score and crease.

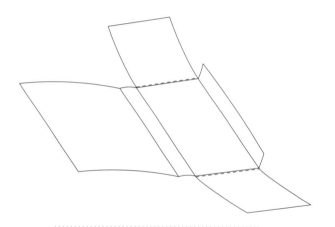

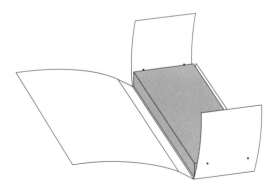

6. Place the horizontal piece in the center of the vertical piece. Score and crease at the head and tail of the horizontal piece.

7. Replace your content, this time marking the thickness with an awl on the flaps of the vertical piece. Set the contents and horizontal piece aside.

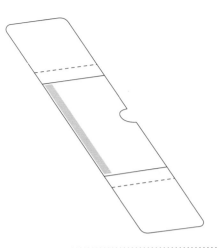

8. Crease the score lines into valley folds. Make a semicircular notch in the center on the right side. Apply double-sided tape at the opposite side from the notch. Round the corners of both pieces, as shown.

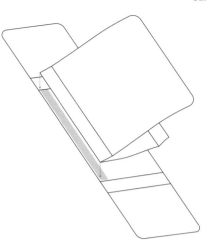

9. Peel the backing paper off the double-sided tape on the vertical piece and place the horizontal piece down, lining up its folded edge with the edge of the vertical piece.

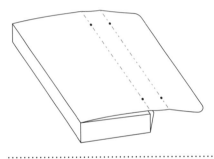

10. Place the contents in the wrapper. Bring the horizontal flap around and mark with an awl for the last two spine folds.

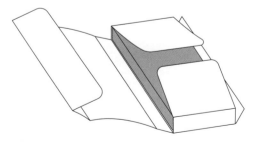

11. Bring the flap back to the left. Score, fold and crease.

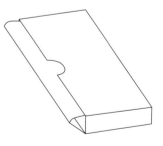

12. To close, insert the flap of the horizontal piece into the gap underneath the semicircular notch.

Biographies

HEDI KYLE was born in Berlin, graduating in 1959 from the Werk-Kunst-Schule in Wiesbaden, Germany, with a degree in graphic design and shortly thereafter emigrated to the United States.

In her capacity as a conservator, she co-founded the Book Preservation Center at the New York Botanical Garden and co-authored one of the first books on library preservation techniques: *Library Materials Preservation Manual.*

Hedi is an honorary member of the Guild of Book Workers and a co-founder, with Gary Frost and Tim Barrett, of the Paper & Book Intensive (PBI), now in its thirtieth year.

Throughout her career as Head Conservator at the American Philosophical Society in Philadelphia, and as an adjunct professor in the Graduate Program for Book Arts and Printmaking at the University of the Arts, Hedi has trained and mentored a generation of conservators and book artists.

Her one-of-a-kind book constructions are in the collections of numerous institutions and individuals and have been the subject of multiple one-person and group exhibitions in the US and abroad.

Today Hedi lives with her husband in the mountains of the Catskills, in upstate New York, and continues to experiment.

ULLA WARCHOL was born in San Francisco and graduated in 1989 from The Cooper Union in New York City with a degree in architecture. After working in the field in the 1990s, Ulla has spent the last two decades developing a multidisciplinary approach to structure. She leans toward a broad exploration of materials and techniques in large-scale works – interiors, buildings and set design – and in small-scale works – books, textiles, fabrication and collaborations with artists.

Ulla now lives in Bucks County, Pennsylvania, with her family, where she divides her time between her wood shop and her studio.

For additional images, tips and videos about our structures and the various techniques we use in this book, visit us at www.artofthefold.com.

Acknowledgments

We wish to express deep gratitude to our editors and designers at Laurence King who gave us freedom and unconditional support throughout the writing of this book: Sophie Drysdale, Philip Contos, Alex Coco, Sarah Hoggett and Caroline Ellerby.

Lucinda Warchol and Jürgen Menningen: you kept us going and on track with valuable feedback, humor and daily sustenance.

For help creating the models in this book, whether it be a beautiful sheet of handmade paper, design ideas or providing a catalyst that sent us off and running, we thank you: Karen Hardy, Casey Ruble and Per Tamsen.

We express special thanks to the people who have been an integral part of developing, researching and testing these structures over the years, and for being longtime friends, colleagues and sources of inspiration: Gary Frost, Denise Carbone, Richard Minsky, Pamela Spitzmueller, Barbara Mauriello, Claire Van Vliet, Barbara Tetenbaum, Julia Miller, Keith Smith, Daniel Kelm, Paul Jackson, Cor Aerssens, Cristina Balbiano d'Aramengo, Benjamin Elbel, Suzanne Schmollgruber, Paul Johnson, Chad Johnson, Bill Hanscom, Rutherford Witthus and Mark Wangberg.

And finally, thank you to Kunihiko Kasahara, author of *Origami Omnibus*, a foundational book on the art of origami that continues to be one of our favorite sources of reference.

LAURENCE KING

Published in 2018
by Laurence King Publishing Ltd
361–373 City Road
London EC1V 1LR
Tel: +4420 7841 6900
Fax: +44 20 7841 6910
Email: enquiries@laurenceking.com
www.laurenceking.com

Reprinted 2019

Design: Alexandre Coco
Copy-editing: Sarah Hoggett
Photography: Paul Warchol

Printed in China

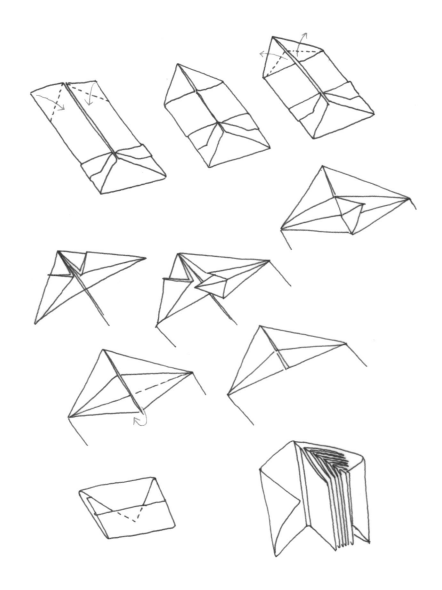

All drawings in this book were hand
drawn from observation by Hedi and then
redrawn by Ulla using Adobe Illustrator.